MW01442399

FAMILY

*A Leadership Fable About the Culture
We All Aspire to Be a Part of*

by
Kent Myers

Copyright © 2024 by Everyday Leadership

Kent Myers

Table of Contents

Foreword *3*
Reflection *6*
The Call *13*
Arrival *21*
Clear the Air *30*
The Walkabout *40*
Trust From Consistency *51*
Support Without Conditions *62*
Grace From Understanding *77*
Contemplating Progress *88*
Honesty and Vulnerability Without Judgment *96*
Accountability With Forgiveness *107*
Lunch Time *116*
Build Each Other Up *126*
The Dugout *137*
The Report *146*
Building the Common Language *153*
Give Trust *161*
Progress Not Perfection *166*
Choose the Right Side *172*
Assume Positive Intent *178*
Positive Gossip *185*
Be Curious *192*
My Work Is Done Here *199*
Discussion Guide *204*

Family

Foreword

Over the past three decades, I have had the privilege of engaging with countless individuals and teams, inviting them to dream of their ideal future culture and distill it into a single, resonant word. Time and again, the answer has echoed back: FAMILY. Now, the reality is that most will quickly follow with the statement, "Well, I don't mean MY family." This one word carries so much meaning to so many.

This recurring theme is not without its critics. In our teams and places of work, the notion of family can be met with skepticism, sometimes dismissed as overly sentimental or impractical in a professional setting. Maybe we believe that in a culture of family there are no boundaries or accountability, or that to be productive and maximize performance we need to completely separate our work from our personal lives.

Yet, the persistent aspiration of this idea of "family" speaks to something profound and deeply ingrained in our collective consciousness.

What is it about the idea of family that captivates us? Why do so many envision their perfect cultural landscape as one that mirrors familial bonds?

This book seeks to unravel these questions and delve into the essence of what people mean when they speak of family in the context of their teams and workplaces by exploring the various dimensions of familial relationships:

> Trust From Consistency
> Support Without Conditions
> Grace From Understanding
> Being Vulnerable Without Judgment
> Accountability With Forgiveness
> and Building Each Other Up

More importantly, this book will offer practical insights and strategies to help transform this widespread aspiration into a tangible reality.

Family

As we embark on this exploration, I invite you to open your mind and heart to the possibilities that a culture of family can bring. Together let us discover how we can create workplaces that not only drive success, but also nourish the human spirit.

Kent Myers

1

Reflection

The thin band of sunlight began to break the horizon of the dawn of a new day as Dr. Henry Tuttle entered his office. Once again, he arrived well before any of the staff or patients. He reached around the corner of the door and flipped on the light switch, illuminating an office that had barely changed in half a century. The back wall was lined with medical books collecting dust. Scattered across the shelves were many

Family

pictures of family, staff and friends—memories of a glorious past.

Henry walked across the room and sat down in an extremely weathered green leather chair. He pulled himself up to a massive oak desk, the one at which his father practiced medicine for 50 years. In his mind he could remember the hero he looked up to sitting in this chair at this desk. As a child, he saw his father as a hero who cured sickness, brought souls into this world and saved lives. It was the life he wanted and the one he had chosen.

As he sat at the desk, he remembered a conversation 42 years earlier with his father as he turned the practice over to him. He remembered his solemn words: "Do no harm and take care of those who care for others. Wherever the art of medicine is loved, there is also a love for humanity."

His father was a brilliant physician who cared deeply about his patients, but also cared for his family and those whom he worked with and considered family. It was a set of values and beliefs that were instilled in Henry at an early age as he watched his father care for this small town, bringing new souls into this world and compassionately taking care of those who left.

He walked over to the bookcase, reached down, and grabbed an old photo album. As he turned the yellowed pages, he saw images of his legacy in front of him; pictures of when his staff banded together during difficult times, like through the challenges of a pandemic, the depressions and economic downturns when few could pay their bills, and that horrific event 10 years earlier when a tornado ravaged a neighboring town and all of the staff united to serve those in need, both physically and mentally.

As he sat and reflected on all of the pictures and memories, tears came to his eyes. They were tears of challenge, but also tears of pride, because he knew that he had built something here—something that was his legacy and would hopefully outlive him.

In this early morning hour, the burden that he had felt for several weeks now weighed heavily on his mind. At the age of 72 and at the prompting of his wife, Elizabeth, Henry had decided to retire and to transition the care of all of

Family

his patients and the operations and culture of his clinic to his youngest daughter, Sara, a very accomplished physician in her own right. She graduated at the top of her class in medical school and spent a residency at Johns Hopkins University. Since then she served in several major hospitals in a variety of roles, but her heart now called her back to this small town to resume the legacy that her grandfather had created.

It had been three months since Sara had arrived back in town and Henry felt uncomfortable transitioning into a life of retirement. He had promised his father that he would "take care of those who care for others." As he looked around the clinic, he didn't recognize the same excitement that he had seen in years past. He didn't see the same smiles on people's faces, hear the same joy in their voices or feel the same excitement for the passion to care for their patients. Henry was very concerned about the culture and about his legacy.

Henry reached back down and picked up the photo album. As he ran his fingers over the weathered pages he thought of every child that he had brought into this world. The scent of old paper and fading ink invoked a sense of nostalgia. In those days, medicine was a dance between doctor and patient; a nuanced waltz of understanding and empathy. House calls were routine and the sound of the doorbell at odd hours was a call to duty rather than an intrusion.

He reminisced about handwritten prescriptions, the elegant script flowing from his pen onto crisp sheets of paper—no electronic signatures, no digital algorithms dictating medication choices. Each prescription was a personalized recommendation, a testament to the doctor's expertise and relationship with the patient. Waiting rooms were filled with the quiet hum of conversation, punctuated by the occasional cough or a child's laughter. There were no smartphones to distract, just people engaged in real conversations, sharing stories and finding solace in the company of others on a similar journey. The pace of those days allowed for thoughtful care. Doctors had the luxury of time—time to listen, to understand, and to connect. The art of medicine flourished, and healing was as much about the human touch as it was about the medications prescribed.

Family

As Henry closed the photo album he couldn't help but smile at the memories that had defined his career. The good old days might be a thing of the past, but the lessons learned and the bonds forged remained eternally present in his heart. The photo pinned to his bulletin board caught his attention: a black-and-white snapshot of Dr. Tuttle and his colleagues, proudly standing in front of the clinic in the town they had served for decades. The camaraderie and shared sense of purpose were palpable in the frozen frame. He thought to himself, "We were a FAMILY."

Dr. Tuttle found this transition to be a phenomenal challenge as he developed his plan to transition patient data, operational processes and technology access. It all seemed easy enough and transactional, but what he did not anticipate was the culture, the *humanity* in the transactions.
He pushed slightly back from his desk and sat on the edge of his leather chair, staring at the closed album that lay in front of him. After a few moments of contemplation, he reached for the phone to make the call.

Kent Myers

2

The Call

Professor John Hill stood by the window of his study gazing out at the brilliant clear sky as the sun glimmered off Lake Michigan, gentle waves lapping against the shore. A smile came to his face as he thought of the next chapter of his life ahead of him. Just three days had passed since he retired from his position at the university, and he had spent most of them in blissful anticipation of the countless leisurely days ahead. The bookshelves once lined with academic journals and textbooks now showcased guides to fly fishing, a new passion he had been eager to pursue.

Retirement had been a long time coming. After nearly four-and-a-half decades of teaching leadership and organizational dynamics, John was ready for a change of pace. He had dreams of spending quiet mornings by the river mastering the delicate art of casting a fly, and afternoons spent reading or writing the mystery novel that had been tumbling around in his brain for years.

John found solace in the idea of retiring to a place that held so many great memories of years gone by. But as John's gaze drifted over the vast expanse of water, his thoughts were abruptly jarred by the ring of the telephone. It was an old-fashioned rotary phone, a relic from another era that John had kept for its nostalgic charm.

"John, it's Henry Tuttle," came the voice of his old friend. John hadn't spoken to Henry in quite a few years, their lives having been on divergent paths since their high school days. "I am really sorry to call so early. I hope I'm not catching you at a bad time."

Family

"Not at all, Henry. What's on your mind?" John replied with a curiosity piqued by the urgency in Henry's tone.

Henry took a deep breath. "That's actually why I'm calling. I'm struggling, John. I'm in the process of handing over the clinic to Sara, but it's proving to be more challenging than I anticipated. I need your help." There was a brief pause on the other end and Henry could almost see John leaning back in his chair, his mind already working on the problem.

"Tell me everything," John said finally. "What's going on?"

Henry launched into the details, explaining how Sara, despite her competence and medical expertise, seemed to be struggling with the cultural aspects of the clinic. She was brilliant and dedicated, but there was a disconnect between her approach and the values the clinic had upheld for so many years. The staff, accustomed to Henry's style of leadership, were finding it difficult to adjust.

"She's trying too hard to make changes," Henry explained. "She's coming in with fresh ideas, which is great, but it's unsettling to everyone. Both the staff and the patients are all feeling the shift, and not necessarily in a good way."

John listened intently, his silence encouraging. When Henry finally finished, John spoke with his voice thoughtful and measured, "Henry, transitions are never easy, especially when it involves something as personal and significant as your clinic. Sara is trying to establish her own identity, which is natural. But it sounds like there needs to be a balance between honoring the past and embracing the future."

Henry sighed. "That's exactly it. But how do we find that balance? I know you are very busy with teaching, but I really need your help here. My father entrusted me with this clinic, and I want to find a way to entrust it to Sara."

John hesitated, glancing at the fly-fishing gear neatly arranged on his desk. He had imagined his retirement as a time of tranquility and personal pursuits, far removed from the bustle and stress of business affairs. Yet, there was something in Henry's voice that struck a chord. It was more

Family

than just a business issue, it sounded like a call for help from an old friend in genuine distress.

"All right, Henry, I'll be happy to help. It has been several years since I have been back to town, so a few fond memories of the past might do me good. I just retired a few days ago, so I have time. How about I come and check things out for myself?"

"Thank you, my friend. You have no idea how much this means to me. I'll see you in a couple of days."

"That sounds good. I'll be there." John agreed, feeling a mix of apprehension, disappointment and resolve to help his friend. He sank back into the worn leather of his armchair, the receiver slipping from his hand. There was a soft click as it returned to the cradle. He had been so looking forward to these days of rest, rivers and relaxation. But now, another call had reached him, one that pulled at a deeper part of his heart.

He stared at the old framed photo on the mantel. It was of his old high school baseball team taken decades earlier when he and Henry were both young and full of wild plans. They had been inseparable back then, tackling life with a camaraderie that felt unbreakable. But time and circumstances had carried them in different directions. Now, Henry needed him.

With a heavy sigh, John stood and moved to the window. The sun was rising, casting a golden hue over the landscape of the lake, a scene that had always brought him solace, and one that he looked forward to viewing every day. He thought of the fishing gear on the desk of his study, the meticulously tied flies and polished rods, all waiting for a retirement that now felt like a postponed dream.

His decision wasn't easy, but it was clear. Duty and loyalty had always been his guiding principles, and they demanded action now more than ever. He walked to the bedroom, pulling an old suitcase from the closet. As he packed, memories of his hometown flooded back—the familiar streets, the old haunts, and the people who had shaped his early years. It had been too long since he'd walked those paths.

Family

The next morning he loaded his suitcase into the back of his old truck, pausing for a moment to look around. The house, the yard, the quiet lake view—all of it would be here when he returned. But for now, he had a different journey to undertake. As he backed out of the driveway, the radio played a tune that seemed fitting: a song about returning home.

The drive was long but familiar, the miles melting away under the tires as memories surfaced with each passing landmark. When he finally arrived in his hometown, the sights and sounds brought a rush of emotions. The town had changed, but its essence remained the same. He drove to the clinic, which looked exactly as he remembered, a testament to the timelessness of small-town life.

Kent Myers

3

Arrival

Professor Hill parked his truck in the small lot in front of the clinic doors. It was the end of the day after a long drive, but John felt like he should stop at least long enough to get the lay of the land and dive into things tomorrow. The clinic, nestled in a quiet corner of the main street, exuded a quaint charm that was inviting and unassuming. A sign above the freshly painted entrance read: "Family Clinic." That sign had hung over those doors for generations.

John stepped through the glass doors, greeted immediately by the familiar odor of antiseptic mixed with the faint aroma of freshly brewed coffee. The waiting area was modest but cozy, with worn leather chairs that had seen years of use and a small table strewn with outdated magazines and children's books. A bulletin board on the wall was adorned with colorful flyers and community announcements, reflecting the clinic's role as a hub for local events and services.

Behind the reception desk, Emily—a cheerful woman with a warm smile—looked up from her computer. "Good morning, Professor Hill," she greeted him, her tone friendly and respectful. "Dr. Tuttle was hoping you might stop by."

"Good afternoon, Emily," John replied, recognizing the receptionist who had been with the clinic for almost as long as Henry had been the primary physician. Even though he had not seen her for years, she looked much the same. She

Family

may have been a bit grayer, but she still had the same smile and kindness.

As he made his way down the familiar hallway, John couldn't help but notice the subtle changes that hinted at the upcoming transition. New medical equipment had been installed, and several rooms had been freshly painted in soothing tones of blue and green. Each examination room was meticulously organized, with charts and instruments neatly arranged. John found Henry in his office. It was a spacious room filled with bookshelves and framed diplomas that testified to countless years of dedication to the medical profession. Henry looked up from a stack of patient files, his face beaming as soon as he saw his old friend.

"John! It's good to see you," Henry said, rising from his chair to embrace him.

"Likewise, Henry. It's been too long," John replied, returning the embrace.

Henry gestured for John to sit. "Thank you for coming. This transition is important to me, and I want to set Sara up for success as my father did for me."

John nodded. "I'm honored to help. How is Sara doing?"

Henry's eyes softened at the mention of his daughter. "She's doing well, but it's a lot to take on. She has the skills and the heart for it, though. The staff loves her, but to be honest, they may not be on board with the pace of change."

John had met Sara Tuttle only a few times, but he had been impressed by her intelligence and empathy. A recent graduate from a prestigious medical school, Sara had returned home to continue the family legacy. As John sat there, he really began to wonder what value he had to offer. He understood the human dynamics of organizational culture and leadership but knew nothing about medical administration and the operations of a clinic.

"Let's take a walk around the clinic," Henry suggested. "I want to show you the changes we've made."

Family

As they strolled through the clinic, Henry pointed out the new additions and upgrades. The pediatric room was now decorated with bright murals of animals and nature scenes, creating a comforting environment for young patients. The staff break room had been renovated, with a coffee machine in the corner that seemed more complex than most of the elaborate medical equipment in the examination rooms and labs. They entered a spacious meeting room where Sara was engaged in a deep discussion with two nurses. She looked up as they entered, her eyes brightening with recognition.

"Professor Hill, it has been a long time!" she said, extending her hand.

"There's the little girl with pigtails I remember! I hear you've been doing an excellent job," John replied, shaking her hand warmly.

Sara smiled modestly. "I'm trying my best. There is just so much to learn and some days I feel like a gerbil on a wheel, running like crazy, but not getting anywhere."

As the last patient of the day was leaving the clinic, Henry said, "Let's all sit down for a moment." The conversation turned to the tension that both Henry and Sara were feeling. The atmosphere in the room changed as if the wind had shifted in the conversation. Henry spoke passionately about the importance of personalized care and the relationships they had built with their patients over the years. He emphasized the clinic's commitment to serving the community, often going above and beyond to ensure that everyone received the care they needed, regardless of their financial situation.

Sara took a deep breath and shared her thoughts in a metaphor. "I thought I would be moving into a new house that I could modernize and make my own, show off my style. Yet it feels like I have walked into a mid-century home with burnt-orange shag carpet and avocado-green fixtures. Not only is no one interested in renovating this house, but there is resistance even to some minor decorative touches."

John listened attentively and could hear the frustration in Sara's voice. He quickly realized that this may have been one of the first times they had articulated this

Family

difference in expectations. At this moment John felt like he was being called to be much more of a therapist than an educator, and it did not sit well with him. However, he did care about this family, this clinic and this community, so he needed to try his very best.

As it grew late in the day and the clinic emptied out, John suggested that they all take the night to ruminate over a few questions:

1. What is the real problem we are trying to solve here?
2. What is the common ground we stand on? What do you believe that you both want and have in common?
3. What does success look like?

John closed the day by saying, "Let's sleep on these and come back tomorrow with open minds, ready to discuss. I think we'll find that the gap is not nearly as wide as what you might imagine."

With that, the trio walked to the front door of the clinic. As Henry locked the door, he turned to John and said, "Thank you, my friend, for coming. It means the world to me." He then turned to look at his daughter and said, "I love my daughter and just want the very best for her, as my father wanted for me."

They all smiled at one another, knowing that words were unnecessary.

Family

4

Clear the Air

The morning sun had just begun to rise, casting a gentle light over the small town. The streets were quiet, with only the occasional car passing by as the town slowly woke up. Professor John Hill walked toward the clinic, his mind focused on the task ahead. Today, he was resuming his meeting with Henry and his daughter, Sara, to address the conflicts that had been brewing within their medical practice during the transition.

Family

As John entered the clinic, he knew one of the first tasks was to somehow figure out how to wrangle a cup of coffee from that elaborate device he had seen in the break room the day before. He stared for a moment, perplexed and intimated by all of the knobs and switches on the coffee machine. He had always gotten by with a simple on/off button.

Just then, Emily, the receptionist, walked in to witness the struggle. "How does a professor with an Ivy League PhD have such a difficult time with a simple machine?" she asked.

"This thing is *anything* but simple. Please, help me!"

"Sure Doc," Emily offered. "Let me help you."

As John took the cup of coffee and headed toward Henry's office, he wondered to himself, *If I struggled this much just to get a cup of coffee, what challenges does the rest of this day hold for me?*

When John reached Henry's office, he poked his head in to see Henry standing behind his desk with a look of weary determination etched on his face. Beside him stood Sara, a picture of modern efficiency and youthful enthusiasm.

"Good morning, John," Henry greeted him, extending a hand. His voice carried the rich timbre of a man who had spent decades comforting the sick and the worried.

"Good morning Henry, Sara," John replied, shaking Henry's hand firmly before turning to Sara. "I appreciate you both coming in early. I know how busy the days can get."

Sara smiled, her eyes sparkling with the same determination that defined her father, but with a modern edge. "We're happy to continue this discussion, Professor Hill. It's important."

They settled into their seats around a small conference table next to the window as the early morning light cast a soft glow. John could sense the tension in the air, the unspoken conflicts that had been festering beneath the surface.

"I understand you've had some challenges." John began, his tone inviting rather than accusatory. "Yesterday, we touched on the broader issues, but today, I want to delve deeper. To do that, I think it's important for us to clarify a few key points. I want to start by addressing those three questions from yesterday that I believe will help guide us through this process: What is it we are trying to solve?

What do you both have in common? What do you both believe? And what does success look like? Let's start with the first question." John paused before asking, "What are we trying to solve? What is the real problem here? Henry, why don't you begin."

Henry leaned back in his chair with a thoughtful expression on his face. "We're trying to find a balance between honoring the past and creating a future, a balance between a personal, patient-centered approach that has defined this clinic for decades and incorporating new methods and technologies. We just need to ensure that as

Sara moves this clinic into the future, we don't lose the essence of what makes this clinic special or lose sight of the humanity amidst the medicine. We have to take care of and protect the culture and the people that make this place great."

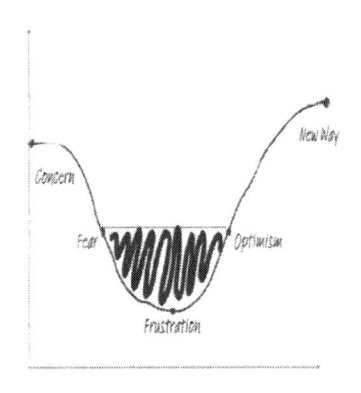

John nodded and turned to Sara. "And you, Sara?"

Sara took a deep breath. "I agree with my father. We need to evolve to stay relevant and provide the best possible care. But I also understand the importance of our clinic's history and the relationships we've built. The challenge is to integrate new methods without disrupting the core values and the culture that our patients and staff hold dear." Sara paused for a moment with a perplexed look on her face. "Actually, I think there is something else we might need to solve: the emotions associated with these changes. Dad keeps saying people are struggling with my changes, but I believe many people just struggle with change." She got out of her chair and walked to the whiteboard to draw a picture. "You see,"

Family

Sara continued, "there is a predictable cycle of emotions that people go through when they deal with change. They begin with some level of concern, which then develops into fear—a fear of the unknown. Then to frustration and the desire to go back to the way things were. But when we stick it out and demonstrate perseverance, we start to see evidence of success and then it simply becomes the way we do things around here." Sara looked up from the whiteboard and said, "I think we are on this journey of the emotions of change after decades of everything being the same."

"That is great," John said. "It sounds like we are not so far apart after all. We are dealing with change and balancing past and future, people and progress. Now, let's move to the second question: What do Henry and Sara have in common, and what do they both believe?"

Henry spoke first, his voice steady. "We both care deeply about the clinic and its future. We believe in providing high-quality medical care and the importance of building strong relationships with our patients. We both want the clinic to thrive and continue serving the community for many years to come. And we both want to continue the legacy that my father—and Sara's grandfather—created here."

Sara nodded. "Absolutely. We both value the trust our patients have in us and we're committed to ensuring that they receive the best care possible. We also believe in the importance of supporting our staff and making sure they feel valued and heard during this transition."

John smiled, sensing a growing understanding between father and daughter. "Excellent. Now, the final question: What does success look like? Henry?"

Henry thought for a moment before saying, "Success, to me, means a clinic where modern technologies and practices enhance our ability to care for patients without losing the personal touch that defines us. It's a place where our staff feel comfortable and confident with the changes, and where our patients continue to feel valued and cared for."

John nodded and turned to Sara. "Sara?"

Family

Sara's eyes lit up with determination. "Success means achieving a seamless integration of new and old. It's about creating an environment where efficiency and innovation support and enhance the patient experience rather than overshadowing it. It's also about building a culture of family and cooperation, where we all serve the same mission together."

John felt a sense of optimism fill the room. The road ahead would be challenging, but with both Henry and Sara committed to working together and guided by these three questions, there was a clear path forward. "Remember," John said, his voice steady and reassuring, "change is a journey, not a destination. It's about finding a balance that honors the past while embracing the future. The common theme I heard today was people and culture. Henry, the words of your father keep coming back to me: Take care of those who care for others."

By now you could begin to hear the hustle and bustle of the clinic coming to life outside of the office walls. You could hear children talking, patient records being retrieved and examination rooms being readied.

As John stood up, he said, "I am going to go on a little walk around town and think about this, but over the next couple of days, I would really like to talk to all of the staff and hear their voices. I would greatly appreciate it if you could arrange a few introductions for me."

Almost simultaneously both Sara and Henry said, "That's a great idea." With a sense of renewed hope and direction, the three walked out of the room to attend to the duties that lay ahead.

Family

5

The Walkabout

Professor John Hill stood at the clinic's front door, taking deep breaths in the crisp, fresh air. The sun was fully up without a cloud in the sky. *What a beautiful day,* he thought to himself. John hadn't been back to the small town he had grown up in for over a decade. As he looked down the Rockwellian Main Street he thought about this topic of change he had just been discussing. His change was inevitable, but just like his view in the moment, he understood the value of many things were consistent, like the simplicity of this small town. That moment gave him an appreciation for the perspectives of both Sara and Henry.

John was not willing to do battle again with the breakroom coffee machine, so he decided instead to stroll down the street to Molly's Café and catch up on all of the town's gossip. On his way, he stopped at the Snoddy's General Store where Mrs. Edith Wallace was arranging a display of fresh produce. This store was iconic and had been there as long as he could remember. He also remembered Mr. Snoddy priding himself on his inventory by saying, "If we ain't got it, you don't need it." Mrs. Wallace, in her late sixties with a warm smile and sharp eyes, greeted him as the doorbell chimed.

"Good morning, Johnny," she said, pausing from her work. "It is so great to see you back in town again!"

"Yes, ma'am, it's good to be back," John replied with a smile. "I'm just back for a few days to help Henry and Sara at the clinic. What do you think about the change?"

Edith sighed, wiping her hands on her apron. "Well, John, you know how it is with change. It's always a bit unsettling at first. Dr. Henry was a rock. His shoes are big ones to fill."

John nodded. "True. But how do you think Sara's doing so far?"

Edith's expression softened. "She's young, yes, but she's got a good head on her shoulders. My granddaughter saw her last week for a bad cough. Sara was patient and thorough, just like her father. I think she's got the makings of a great doctor, given time."

"That's reassuring," John said. "Do you think the community will come around?"

Edith chuckled. "Oh, they will. People here can be stubborn, but they're also fair. Once they see she's capable, they'll accept her. It's just a matter of proving herself. I am sure it was similar to Henry and his dad."

Family

John thanked Edith and continued his walk, her words echoing in his mind. A block later, John passed the post office. Outside Mr. Timothy Harper, the postman, was sorting mail for delivery. Timothy, with his gray hair and friendly demeanor, had been the town's postman for over four decades and knew everyone by name. He and John had grown up and played baseball together.

"Morning, Tim," John greeted him.

"Hey, good morning, Scooter!" Timothy replied, looking up from his work. "Scooter" was a nickname that John had not been called in years, and one that he was not particularly enamored with. "What are you doing back in town?" asked Tim. "I'm not aware of a class reunion or a new university coming to town."

"I am just back to help Henry and Sara at the clinic for a few days. I am actually a whole five days into retirement as a Professor. What do you think about Henry's retirement and him turning the clinic over to Sara?"

Timothy paused, his brow furrowing in thought. "She's young, that's for sure. But she's got the same sharp mind as her father and grandfather. She's already handled a few tricky cases. Folks are cautious, but I think she's got potential. What concerns me is whether she can handle the pressure and the community's expectations. She clearly knows her stuff, but John didn't just see us as patients, he saw us as *family*. Henry and his father are responsible for bringing half of the population of this town into the world."

John leaned against the post office's wooden railing. "That's a great point. Do you think people will give her a fair chance?"

Timothy nodded slowly. "Yes, I do. People might be skeptical, but they're also supportive once they see someone's earnestness. Dr. Henry earned their trust over years and Sara will have to do the same, and I believe she will."

Their conversation lingered on the challenges of transitioning leadership and the weight of community expectations. John felt a growing sense of optimism tempered

Family

with the understanding of the hurdles ahead.

As the morning wore on, John made his way to Molly's Café, a popular spot known for its superior service and delicious food. The café was bustling this morning with activity, but Molly, the café's owner, noticed John and came out from behind the counter to see him as he settled into a corner table.

"Professor Hill! What a pleasant and unexpected surprise to see you back in town today!" she exclaimed, wiping her hands on a towel.

"I thought I'd treat myself to a late breakfast. I would never come into town without stopping by for a cup of your delicious coffee and a hearty breakfast," John replied. "I am back in town helping Henry and Sara at the clinic and thought I might as well stop by to catch up on all of the town gossip."

Molly poured him a steaming cup of coffee and set in front of him a plate of scrambled eggs, toast, and bacon. "Well, you've come to the right place. People talk about everything here."

John took a sip of his coffee, savoring the rich aroma. "So, what's the latest scoop in town?"

Molly pulled up a chair and sat down across from him, taking a rare break from her busy routine. "Honestly, John, it's Henry's retirement. Some people are nervous about the change. Dr. Henry was practically a legend around here. But others are optimistic. Sara's got new ideas and techniques. She's already impressed a few of the regulars who were initially skeptical. What I am most concerned about is the culture of the clinic. Several nurses and members of the staff have been talking over the past few weeks. I hear statements like, 'I miss the old days' and 'Things are really going to be different now, this feels like a business.'"

John nodded thoughtfully. "It sounds like she's on the right track. It's just a matter of taking time and earning trust."

Molly agreed. "Yes, but change is hard for most people. Sara has the skills, no doubt about that, but there is

Family

more to caring for people than dispensing band-aids and aspirin. It's her compassion and understanding that will win people over, she just needs the chance to show it. There are some great people who work at that clinic, I hope they don't get lost in the shuffle."

John finished his meal, grateful for the candid conversations. As he left the café and continued his walk, he felt more confident in the clarity of the battle ahead. John thought, *If this change was so apparent to the people in the community, what must those working in the clinic be feeling right now?*

By the time he returned to the clinic, the sun was high in the sky and the parking lot was full. As John walked through the front door he saw a packed waiting room. In that moment, John realized how critical this clinic was to the town. He understood that he was not just here helping his old friend, but helping the town he grew up in and loved.

Just a few steps in the door, John saw Sara approaching. "So, did you hear all of the gossip from Molly's?"

John laughed. "Even after all of these years, there is never a shortage of gossip and opinions in that little café!"

Sara told John that she was ready for him to talk to the staff as he had requested. She had set up a makeshift office in one of the back hallways where it would be quiet and people would feel comfortable talking. Sara walked him down a hallway and flipped on a light switch. What appeared from the darkness was what John took to be a hurriedly converted storage closet with a table and a couple of chairs.

"This will do," he said. John could very much appreciate the effort to try to create accommodations on very short notice. While it was small and utilitarian, it was also well-lit and inviting, even down to the small potted plant that he was sure had been placed in the corner just minutes earlier. "Actually, this is perfect," John said. "Thank you so much, Sara, for putting this together so quickly."

Sara, with one hand on the doorknob and a foot out the door, said, "As you can see from the lobby, this is going to be a very busy day. I don't have a schedule for you, but I have asked all of the staff to stop by when they have a few

Family

minutes. I think they are excited to talk with you. Let me know if you need anything else. Thank you again." With that, Sara got back to her patient care duties.

John sat down at the table with his leather journal open as he contemplated and absorbed all he had already heard that morning as he awaited his first visitor.

Kent Myers

6

Trust from Consistency

As John Hill sat at the table awaiting a visitor, he felt the familiar tugging of fatigue at his eyes. With a sigh, he decided to make a quick stop at the clinic break room for a much needed cup of coffee before heading back to the small office for interviews.

Kent Myers

Pushing open the door to the break room, he was greeted by the hum of the fluorescent lights and the hum of the refrigerator. His eyes immediately landed on the coffee machine—a sleek, modern contraption that seemed more suited for a sci-fi movie than a medical clinic. Professor Hill approached it with cautious optimism. This time he would not be defeated.

The machine had a digital interface with an overwhelming array of options: espresso, cappuccino, latte, macchiato, Americano and more. He just wanted a simple black coffee, but the touch screen demanded a decision on the type of beans, cup size, the water temperature and even how finely ground the beans had to be. He hesitated, poking at the screen, hoping to find a "regular coffee" button, but such simplicity was not reasonable to expect.

After several frustrating minutes of navigating menus and sub-menus, he finally managed to select what he thought was a plain coffee option. He pressed the button and the machine whirred to life, making all sorts of impressive noises. After a moment, a small trickle of dark liquid began to pour into his cup. He watched with a mix of relief and suspicion as

Family

the cup filled up halfway before the machine beeped and stopped abruptly. He sighed, realizing that he had selected an espresso shot instead of a full cup of coffee.

Resigned to his fate, he picked up the half-full cup and turned around, hoping to find solace in the peaceful ambiance of the break room. As he took a sip, he noticed the large bulletin board on the wall adorned with colorful pictures and notes. Drawn in by the cheerful display, he walked over to examine it more closely. There were pictures of patients and employees, birthday celebrations, holiday parties and team-building events. Everyone looked happy and connected, their smiles radiating warmth and camaraderie. In the center of the board a large sign read: "We Are *Family*."

Professor Hill smiled softly, sensing the comfort and belonging. He recognized a few faces from his interactions in the clinic, remembering their stories and the times they had shared brief but meaningful conversations. The sign and the photos served as a poignant reminder of the community that surrounded him, even in a place as busy and chaotic as this clinic in transition.

Kent Myers

As he stood there sipping his strong espresso shot, he realized that despite the complexity of the coffee machine and the frustrations of the day, he was part of something much larger at play here. Despite what may be the frustrations of the current changes, the bulletin board was a testament to the connections and relationships that made the clinic a true family; a place where everyone looked out for each other.

With a renewed sense of appreciation, Professor Hill finished his drink, feeling a bit more energized. He took one last look at the bulletin board, letting the warmth of the images wash over him before heading back to the small office the anticipated conversations.

As John sat down in his chair, he heard a sound on the other side of the office. He glanced up as the door creaked open. There in the doorway was Nurse Judy Walters. Her auburn hair was pulled back into a tight ponytail and the tired lines around her eyes spoke of another long day. She smiled weakly at John and sank into the chair opposite him, her shoulders sagging with an invisible weight.

Family

"Long day?" John asked gently, his eyes full of empathy.

Judy sighed, running a hand through her hair. "Aren't they all?"

John nodded slowly as he took a sip from his cup. "I suppose. Sounds like the clinic has changed so much recently that it's almost hard to keep up." John set his cup down, leaning forward slightly. "I understand you've been with the clinic for quite a long time."

"Yes, 27 years," she answered with a nod. "It's been my second home."

"I can imagine," Professor Hill said. "You must have seen quite a few changes over the years. Could you tell me about the recent changes that have troubled you?"

A wistful look crossed Judy's face. "John, I used to be able to trust that things would be constant. It was our anchor, you know? The routines, the familiar faces and the way we all knew each other's quirks and habits. It made us family." Judy sighed, her gaze drifting momentarily to the wall. "It's the loss of consistency, Professor. For so many years we had a way of doing things that everyone could rely on. Patients knew what to expect from us. There was a certain rhythm to our days."

"Consistency in what, exactly?" Hill prompted gently.

"In everything," Judy said, her voice steady. "There was consistency in how we did things, how we treated each other and how we reacted to situations. We had routines and protocols that everyone followed. It created a sense of reliability and trust, not just the staff, but also among our patients. In preparation for this meeting, I made a list of things I could place my trust in."

Judy opened the notebook and turned a page so John could read the cleanly printed words.

Consistency I Could Trust

- ***We show up as ourselves*** People are people, in behavior and actions, regardless of the situation they are in.

Family

- ***We are true to our word***   Simply put, we do what they say we will do. We honor our commitments.

- ***No one is "flavor of the day"***   We are not swayed by the current trend of thought or those who change direction like the wind. We know what we believe and live consistently in those beliefs.

- ***We don't make excuses!***   We refrain from saying, "I forgot," or "I didn't have time to…" We hold ourselves accountable.

- ***We communicate consistently***   This eliminates confusion or misunderstandings and avoids hurt feelings. We don't avoid difficult conversations, don't ignore calls or messages, and always promptly reply to texts and emails.

- ***We must not merely be 'people pleasers'***   We should have the courage to say 'no.' If we can't follow through, we'll be seen as unreliable, and everyone involved will be worse off. Don't overpromise and underdeliver. Dr. Henry Tuttle always said, "Either keep your promises or do not make them."

- **We only say it if we mean it** We need to make sure anything we say is something we genuinely believe or feel. Being consistent means being honest and truthful.

- **We constantly express gratitude** We show how much we appreciate the efforts of others, nurturing our connections.

Professor Hill scribbled in his notebook, nodding. "That is a great explanation and a great list, but can you give me some specific examples?"

"Sure," Judy said. "Take our morning meetings, for instance. For years we'd start our day with a brief meeting to go over the day's schedule, discuss any issues and offer each other support. We also shared stories about our lives, our kids and our families. It set the tone for the day. Lately, those meetings have been sporadic and sometimes canceled without notice. It leaves everyone feeling disjointed and unprepared." She paused, collecting her thoughts. "Then there's the way we interact with our patients. They used to know exactly what to

Family

expect from us because we were all on the same page. Now, with new policies and changes in staff, patients are often confused. They're not sure who to talk to or what the procedures are anymore."

Hill tapped his pen on the notebook. "And how has this affected the staff?"

"It's been hard," Judy admitted, her voice softening. "We used to have a strong sense of camaraderie. We trusted each other because we knew we all operated under the same principles. Now, with so much inconsistency, it's like we're all on edge. We're not sure what to expect."

"How do you think this consistency was maintained before?" Hill asked.

"Leadership," Judy said firmly. "Henry valued and upheld our routines and protocols. They understood the importance of consistency for both staff morale and patient care. He led by example, and we followed."

Kent Myers

Professor Hill made a final note before looking up. "Judy, thank you for sharing this with me. It's clear that consistency is very important to you and to the well-being of the clinic. I hope we can find a way to restore that."

"I hope so, too, Professor," Judy said with a faint smile. "For all our sakes."

As she left the room, Professor Hill pondered her words. Consistency, it seemed, was the glue that held this clinic together. His task now was to understand how it had unraveled and, more importantly, how it could be mended.

Professor Hill watched as Nurse Judy left the room, her shoulders squared against the weight of her concerns. The small clinic's office, though modest, bore the signs of importance—a space where years of dedication and service had been planned and executed with care. Hill turned his attention back to his notes. The phrase **"Trust in Consistency"** was underlined heavily at the top of the page.

Family

7

Support without Conditions

With one interview down and many more to go, John thought that he would stretch his legs and see what was going on in the lobby. He could hear the commotion in the waiting room as he drew closer.

John passed the waiting area where families sat in various states of anticipation. A mother rocked her restless toddler, whispering soothing words in his ear. An elderly man leaned heavily on his cane; his eyes closed as he rested. The atmosphere was a mix of hope and anxiety; each person

Family

clinging to the promise of relief and answers.

In one corner of the waiting room a young woman sat alone, her face pale and drawn. She glanced around nervously, her fingers twisting a tissue into tight knots. John recognized her as Amy, one of the waitresses at Molly's Café. He didn't know Amy was a regular patient who was battling a chronic illness. Despite her frequent visits, the fear in her eyes never seemed to diminish.

Just then, Emily, one of the clinic's receptionists, approached Amy with a warm smile. "Amy, it's good to see you," she said, her voice gentle. "I know you're here for your follow-up appointment, but I wanted to check in with you first. How are you feeling today?"

Amy's eyes filled with tears and she quickly looked down, embarrassed by her emotion. "I'm scared, Emily. I know I should be used to this by now, but... it's just so hard. I know I am seeing Dr. Sara today and I am a bit anxious. I know she is an accomplished doctor, but her father has cared for me for years. I trust him."

Kent Myers

Emily reached out, resting a comforting hand on Amy's shoulder. "It's okay to be scared. You're not alone in this. We're all here to help you through it. Please know that Dr. Sara is an outstanding doctor and a kind and wonderful person. She isn't just my doctor, but my friend. This town will be well served for decades."

Neither Emily nor Amy could see that Dr. Sara was standing within a close enough distance to hear their conversation. John, watching the scene, made eye contact with Dr. Sara. With a look of humility and sadness, she half smiled at John and then glanced away.

As John watched this simple yet profound interaction, he was struck by the power of human connection. In a place where clinical precision and medical expertise were paramount, the real heart of the clinic lay in moments like these. It was in the way people looked out for one another, offering strength and solace in times of need—the humanity behind the appointments.

Family

As Emily walked back around the counter and behind the glass partition of the lobby, she saw Dr. Sara. "Ohhh, Dr Tuttle, I didn't see you there. You startled me."

Sara Tuttle smiled and said, "Emily, I heard your conversation with Amy. You were very compassionate. It was kind, not only in the way you comforted Amy in this difficult time, but also in what you said about me. Did you mean it?"

Emily smiled and answered, "Yes, I want you to be successful. Please know I always have your back."

John walked back to the small office still thinking about the encouraging example of humanity he had just witnessed. As soon as he sat down in his chair he heard the creak of the door. As he looked up, there was Emily's smiling face.

"Good afternoon, Professor Hill. I understand that you wanted a few minutes with each of us. Is now a good time?" Emily asked.

"Absolutely," John replied. "This is not an inquisition. I know there is a lot of change going on here and I just want to hear from everyone and see how they are doing. By the way, Emily, I saw your interaction with that patient in the waiting room. Your kindness was inspirational. It was amazing how your kind words of support for Dr. Sara calmed her nerves. You inspired me. So, tell me, how do you feel about all these changes?"

Emily took a deep breath, her gaze drifting as she recalled the past. "There was a time not too long ago when this clinic felt like more than just a place of work, it felt like a family. We all had each other's backs and provided unconditional support no questions asked. It didn't matter if you were a doctor, a nurse or a receptionist like me."

"Can you give me an example?" John asked, leaning in slightly.

"Sure," Emily nodded. "I remember a particularly busy flu season a couple of years ago. The waiting room was packed every day, and we were all exhausted. One evening I

Family

stayed late to help sort out the next day's appointments. Dr. Henry noticed I was here after hours. Without a word, he rolled up his sleeves and started helping me. We worked side by side for hours, chatting about our families and favorite books. It wasn't just the work we shared, but a connection."

John scribbled down some notes, his pen moving swiftly across the paper. "That's a wonderful example of camaraderie. Was that a common occurrence?"

"Absolutely," Emily said with a smile. "Another time one of our nurses, Margret, had a personal emergency. Her daughter was hospitalized suddenly, so she had to leave in the middle of her shift. Instead of leaving her patients unattended or scrambling to find a replacement, another nurse named Patty and I covered her responsibilities. I handled some of the simpler tasks like checking in patients while Patty took on the medical duties. We all pitched in without a second thought because we knew Margret needed to be with her family."

John nodded appreciatively. "It sounds like there was a strong sense of mutual support."

"There really was," Emily agreed, her smile fading slightly. "But things have changed recently. It feels like everyone is more isolated now, more focused on their own roles and less on supporting each other."

"Why do you think that is?" John asked gently.

Emily hesitated, choosing her words carefully. "I think part of it is the pressure. We're busier than ever and there are always new regulations, new technologies to learn. Then there is just the tension of the transition and the fear of the unknown. It's like we're running on a treadmill that keeps speeding up. People are stressed, and when you're stressed, it's hard to think about anyone else's problems."

"That makes sense," John said thoughtfully. "Do you have any other memories that stand out from the times when the clinic felt more unified?"

Family

"Yes," Emily said, her eyes lighting up once more. "There was a time when we organized a surprise birthday party for one of our janitors, Mr. Lee. He was always so kind, quietly doing his work and never asking for recognition. We all chipped in for a cake, decorations and a gift. Seeing the look on his face when he walked into the break room and saw everything was priceless. It wasn't about the party itself, but the fact that we all came together to show appreciation for someone who might otherwise go unnoticed."

"That's a beautiful story, Emily," John said, his voice filled with genuine admiration. "It seems those moments of connection and support were what made the clinic special."

"They were," Emily agreed. "I miss that feeling. I miss knowing that no matter how tough the day got, we were all in it together and we had each other's backs. Now, it feels like everyone is just struggling to get through their challenges on their own."

John nodded, finishing his notes. "Thank you for sharing these stories, Emily. They paint a vivid picture of what this clinic used to be and what it could be again. Your insights are invaluable."

Emily smiled, a flicker of hope in her eyes. "Thank you, Professor Hill. I hope you can help us find our way back to that sense of community."

John stood, extending his hand. "I will do my best. And I hope you'll continue to be a beacon of warmth and support here. It's people like you who make all the difference. You make a greater impact than you realize."

As John watched Emily return to the receptionist deck, he couldn't help but reflect on Emily's words. The strength of a community lies in its ability to support each member unconditionally. He resolved to use Emily's stories as a foundation for his research, aiming to uncover the keys to fostering a more connected and supportive workplace. He flipped back a few pages in his notebook and underlined the phrases.

We support each other unconditionally. We had each other's backs.

Family

John glanced down at his watch, a 100-year-old Panerai that had been once been his grandfather's before being passed down to his father and then to John. As John reflected on that for a moment, this word "family" that he had heard all day kept coming back to him.

It was late enough in the afternoon, and with a mixture of satisfaction and exhaustion, he thought the fresh perspective of a new day tomorrow might bring some additional clarity to all that he had heard from staff and the community. John got up from his chair, approached the door, and with a loud click, shut off the lights in the office.

As he entered the hallway, he sensed the clinic had begun to settle into the late afternoon rhythm, as the bustle of patients dwindled and the corridors grew quieter. As he walked through the hushed hallway, the sound of his footsteps echoed faintly off the polished floors. Passing by the offices, John's gaze wandered aimlessly until it landed on a scene that made him stop in his tracks. There, through the half-open door of Dr. Sara Tuttle's office, he saw her sitting at her desk, her head buried in her hands. The sight was so out of character for the usually composed and confident Sara that he couldn't ignore it.

He knocked gently on the doorframe, the sound barely more than a whisper. "Sara, are you all right?"

Startled, Sara lifted her head before quickly brushing away a stray tear. Her eyes, red and weary, met his with a forced smile. "Oh, John. I didn't hear you coming. I'm fine, just... a long day."

John stepped into the office, closing the door softly behind him. "You don't look fine. What's going on?"

Sara sighed, the weight of the day pressing heavily on her shoulders. "It's just been one of those days where everything seems to be going wrong. Every patient felt like a challenge I couldn't meet, every decision second-guessed. And then, to top it off, I overheard a conversation earlier that shook me more than I expected."

John pulled a chair closer and sat down, giving her his full attention. "Do you want to talk

Family

about it?"

Sara hesitated, then nodded. "I overheard Emily talking about me earlier today. She was speaking to one of our recurring patients, and at first, I thought it was just the usual clinic gossip. But it wasn't. She was saying so many kind things about me, even calling me a friend."

John smiled, a hint of pride in his eyes. "That sounds like something Emily would say. She looks up to you a lot."

"Yes, but that's not all," Sara continued. "Emily went on to say that she believed in me. She didn't know I was listening, but her words... they gave me a perspective I'd lost; a perspective I needed."

John leaned back, contemplating her words. "It sounds like Emily has a lot of respect for you. And from what I've seen, it's well-deserved."

Sara's eyes softened. "Hearing her support me without knowing I was there, it was... humbling. I've been so caught up in my own struggles with this transition that I forgot how much my actions can affect others. Emily's faith in me reminded me of why I chose this path in the first place."

John nodded thoughtfully. "It's easy to forget our own impact when we're bogged down by daily challenges. But it's clear that you're making a difference, not just with your patients, but with your colleagues, too."

Sara took a deep breath, feeling the weight lifting slightly from her shoulders. "I want to be that person that Emily spoke of, that she said such positive things about. I want to be the kind of mentor and friend that Emily sees in me. If she can see that in me, even when I'm doubting myself, then maybe I'm doing something right."

"You're doing a lot of things right, Sara," John said, his voice warm with reassurance. "And if you ever need a reminder, just think about what Emily said. You're not alone in this. Many people support you and have your back." At that moment, John thought back to those words he had just underlined moments ago.

A small smile crept across Sara's face, genuine this time. "Thank you, John. Sometimes we just need someone to remind us of our own worth."

With those words, John got up and placed a hand on Sara's shoulder and said, "It was a good day today; we are gonna get there. I'll see you tomorrow."

As John opened the door to leave the clinic, the warmth of the setting sun hit his face. He thought to himself, *It absolutely was a good day, and this is a special place.*

Kent Myers

8

Grace From Understanding

Professor John Hill was an early riser by habit. The morning was his sanctuary—a time when the world was quiet, and he could gather his thoughts. This particular morning he decided to take a walk. The air was crisp and cool, the first light of dawn casting a gentle glow over the small town. As he strolled through the familiar streets, his path and his thoughts naturally led him toward the clinic. With each step he thought more about the conversations he'd had with the staff the day before and both the complexities and the simplicity of the transition that lay ahead. He also began to wonder if many of the challenges that they were facing now were also encountered when Henry's father handed the clinic over to *him*.

As he approached the clinic, John noticed a light in one of the windows. It seemed unusual for anyone to be there at that hour, so his curiosity was piqued. Approaching the entrance, he found the door slightly ajar. He stepped inside and made his way down the hallway, his footsteps echoing throughout the empty building.

In the dim light of the corridor John saw the familiar figure of Dr. Henry Tuttle hunched over his desk, surrounded by stacks of papers. Henry looked up as John entered, a weary smile crossing his face.

"John, you're up early," Henry said, rubbing his eyes.

"I could say the same about you," John replied, pulling up a chair. "Couldn't sleep?"

Family

Henry sighed and leaned back in his chair. "No, not really. I still have a lot of concerns about handing this clinic over to Sara. She's more than capable, but... well, you know how it is."

John nodded. "It's a big change, both professionally and personally. You have built something great here and I'm sure it's hard to let that go and hand it over to someone else—*anyone* else, let alone your own daughter—but she will do well."

Henry smiled, though it didn't quite reach his eyes. "I know. It's just... I've been thinking about how things have changed and how they haven't.

"Yesterday, I had interviews with Emily and Nurse Judy."

Henry's eyebrows raised slightly. "How did it go?"

"Emily's such a kind and caring soul, and Nurse Judy," John said softly, "she really cares about this place and these people. Both have such passion for the work here."

Henry nodded thoughtfully. "That's good to hear. You know, John, one of the secrets to this place's success over the past few decades is that people here really know each other. Not in an intrusive way, but in a caring way. We've built a community where we understand what's going on in each other's lives."

In Henry's wise way, he continued, "Henry David Thoreau once asked, 'Could a greater miracle take place than for us to look through each other's eyes for an instant?' Every person has a story; there's a reason behind who they are and what they've done, but we're usually not privy to that information."

"The difference between judgment and empathy is knowing someone's story."

John leaned forward, listening intently. Henry continued, "When things get tough, people here give each other grace. They remember that behind every mistake or shortcoming, there's a human being. Like when Judy's

Family

husband was ill a few years back, everyone pitched in to cover her shifts. No one questioned it; they just did it because they cared."

John nodded as Henry continued. "And when Emily's daughter was born prematurely, the whole clinic rallied around her. People brought meals and took over her workload. It was like an extended family." Henry smiled. "And it's not just the big things. It's the little acts of kindness that matter, too. Remember old Mrs. Finch? She used to bring cookies every Friday. It was a small thing, but it meant so much to everyone."

John laughed. "Those cookies were legendary. And it's those small things that build the fabric of this place. It's why it feels like home."

Henry sighed again, this time with a hint of relief. "That's what I'm hoping Sara will understand. It's not just about the medicine or the procedures, it's about the people—the relationships, the trust we've built. That's the real heart of this clinic."

Henry's gaze shifted to the window where the morning light was beginning to filter through. "John, I worry that with Sara taking over, this culture we've built might disappear. It's not that I doubt her abilities. It's just... maintaining that sense of understanding and grace isn't easy."

John listened quietly, sensing the depth of Henry's concern. "Why do you think it might change?" he asked gently.

Henry sighed, his shoulders slumping a bit. "Times are different now. The world moves faster. People are more focused on efficiency and results. It's not that these things aren't important, but there's a risk of losing sight of the human element. Sara is excellent, but she's coming into a different world from the one we started in."

John considered this for a moment. "You're right, Henry. Times have changed. But the essence of what you've built here—the relationships, the empathy—those are timeless values. If anyone can bridge the old and the new, it's Sara."

Family

Henry gave a slight nod. "I hope so, but I worry she might feel pressured to make changes that align with modern expectations, potentially at the expense of our core values."

"I know you have talked about the transition, but have you talked to her about this specifically?" John asked.

Henry shook his head. "Not directly. I don't want to make her feel like she's under my shadow or that she can't innovate. But I do want her to understand how important this culture is."

John leaned forward and said in a steady and reassuring tone, "Henry, you need to share these concerns with Sara. She deserves to know what's important to you and why. You've instilled those values in her, but she needs to hear it from you directly. Trust her to carry them forward in her way."

Henry looked thoughtful. "You're right. I've been so focused on the transition itself that I haven't really opened up to her about my deeper fears."

John smiled. "It's never too late. And I think you'll find that Sara understands more than you realize. She's seen the way this clinic operates. She's experienced support and kindness. She'll find her own way to uphold that legacy." John reached out and placed a reassuring hand on Henry's shoulder. "She's seen it firsthand. She grew up with it. And with your guidance, she'll carry it forward. Your leadership has cast an amazing shadow on this place and it will be your legacy."

Henry looked at John, gratitude in his eyes. "Thanks, John. I needed that." As the first rays of the sun peeked through the window, Henry stood up and stretched. "I suppose we should get ready for the day."

John nodded, standing as well. "Indeed. Let's see what this day brings."

As they walked through the now brightly lit corridor they could hear additional echoes of footprints through the hallway and the hum of equipment stirring to life. John knew that this was going to be a busy day. He hoped to conclude all

Family

of his interviews that day and hear all of the voices that were articulating the aspirations of the clinic's future.

As the sun was rising, so was his optimism in the people and the future. Just as John rounded the corner, his faith in humanity was confirmed. Standing there with a cup of black coffee in her hand was Emily, the receptionist. With a smile on her face she exclaimed, "Good morning, Professor. Thank you for the great conversation yesterday. I wanted to get your day started off right and not make you go three more rounds with that malicious coffee maker. Here is a cup just the way you like it: hot and black. Have a great day and know that I appreciate you."

As John stepped into the small office he sat down in his chair, opened his tattered briefcase and pulled out his journal. He began to capture the conversation that morning. With pen in hand he mused over a word he had heard several times already that morning: **grace**. John found this word interesting. He thought to himself, grace is both a *noun* and a *verb*—a feeling and an action. It can be interchanged with giving someone a chance, time, the ability to make mistakes without punishment… and forgiveness. Grace is a powerful concept if we really take the time to seriously contemplate it. When we take time to get to know each other, we understand each other. When we understand each other, we can respond with kindness and empathy, not judgment or assumptions.

At that moment, John took a sip of coffee, set the cup down, picked up his pen and wrote on the blank page: **"Grace from Understanding."**

Family

9

Contemplating Progress

Professor John Hill sat in the clinic office, a blend of anticipation and contemplation swirling in his mind. He was waiting to conduct his final interviews, but his thoughts kept drifting back to the conversations he'd had over the past 24 hours. The clinic had a warmth and camaraderie that he hadn't encountered elsewhere. All those he met shared a piece of

Family

this puzzle that formed the clinic's unique culture. He opened his leather journal and began flipping through the pages.

The first set of notes he came upon was from Judy Walters. The previous day, Nurse Judy had shared an invaluable insight that she called "Trust from Consistency." Judy had spoken with quiet conviction, her eyes reflecting years of experience and dedication. "It's the consistency in the office," she had said, "how we act, how we treat each other, and how we serve our patients. This consistency creates trust because everyone knows how things will consistently occur. It's not just about medical care, but about reliability. Patients come here because they know they will be treated with respect and professionalism every single time."

John remembered nodding, feeling the weight of her words. Consistency wasn't just a habit here, it was a cornerstone of trust and a foundation upon which relationships were built and maintained.

As he got to the bottom of the page, he saw the underlined words: "Trust from Consistency." On a new page, he began to draw a small diagram. His first image was a small circle with the words "Trust from Consistency" inside.

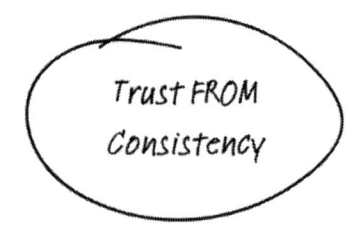

Trust FROM Consistency

John continued to leaf through his journal and came to the next interview. Later that day he'd had a conversation with Emily, the clinic receptionist. She was the first face people saw when they entered the clinic, and she exuded a sense of warmth and welcome. Emily spoke about "Support without conditions." She recounted stories of how the staff looked out for each other, creating a safety net of support that was always there, regardless of the circumstances. "We have each other's backs," she had said with a smile. "Whether it's covering a shift at the last minute, helping with a challenging patient or just being there to listen when someone needs to talk, we support each other unconditionally. It's like a family here."

Family

John was struck by the depth of her sentiment. In many workplaces, support came with strings attached or was doled out sparingly—even begrudgingly. Here, it flowed freely, fostering a sense of belonging and mutual respect.

As he looked at the bottom of his page of notes, he saw the underlined words, "Support Without Conditions," and added these words to his diagram.

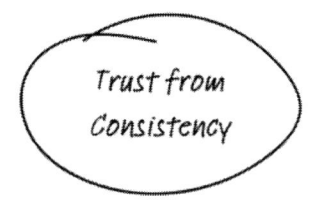

(Support Without Conditions)

(Trust from Consistency)

As he turned more pages, he came to the notes from that morning. His conversation with Dr. Henry Tuttle had added another layer to his understanding. Dr. Tuttle spoke of

"Grace from Understanding." He emphasized the importance of knowing each other beyond professional roles. "We care about what's happening in each other's lives," he had said. "We assume positive intent and give each other grace. When someone is having a tough day, we don't jump to conclusions. We understand and support them, giving them the grace they need to get through it."

John found this perspective both refreshing and profound. In a world often quick to judge, extending grace through understanding felt like a rare and precious gift. It reminded him that empathy and compassion were vital in any setting, especially in one as demanding as a medical clinic.

As he sat in the office, waiting for his interviews, John's thoughts wandered to the picture wall in the break room where a single word was prominently displayed in the center: "Family." It all made sense now—trust from consistency, support without conditions and grace from understanding—these principles were the threads that wove the fabric of this family together. They created an environment where everyone felt valued, supported and understood.

Family

John picked up his pen and added it to his diagram.

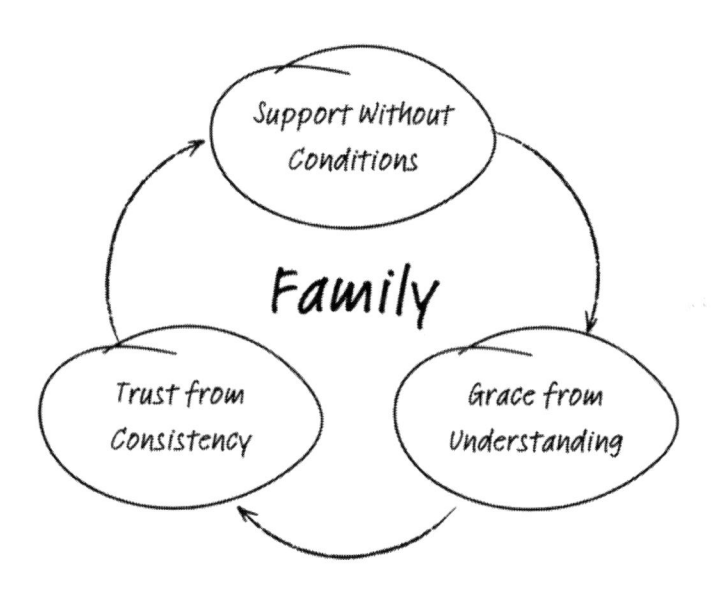

```
         ┌─────────────────┐
         │ Support Without │
         │   Conditions    │
         └─────────────────┘
                Family
   ┌──────────────┐   ┌──────────────┐
   │  Trust from  │   │  Grace from  │
   │  Consistency │   │ Understanding│
   └──────────────┘   └──────────────┘
```

John realized that this clinic wasn't just a workplace, it was a community and a sanctuary where both staff and patients found solace and strength. The word "Family" encapsulated the essence of what he had experienced here. It was a reminder that in this clinic, they weren't just colleagues, they were family—bound by a shared commitment to care, respect, and support for one another.

He took a deep breath, feeling a sense of calm and purpose. The final interviews were imminent, but John already knew that he wanted to be part of this family. The conversations he had had and the principles he had learned resonated deeply. He felt a profound respect for the culture they had developed here and now he understood the beliefs, attitudes and behaviors that his friend, Henry, wanted to protect.

As the door to the office opened, John heard, "Professor Hill, is now a good time to talk?" As John looked up, he saw the clinic's medical assistant, Jason Stewart, standing in front of him. Jason was the son of one of John's childhood friends.

John replied, "Goodness, Jason, you are not the little boy I remembered. Of course, now is a good time. Please come in."

Family

10

Honesty and Vulnerability without Judgment

Jason entered the room, his body language communicating uncertainty and nervousness. He timidly stepped into the room and closed the door behind him, taking care to avoid any direct eye contact. John sensed his unease and stood to extend a welcoming handshake.

"Thank you for agreeing to talk with me, Jason," John began, adjusting his glasses and opening his notebook. "I'm particularly interested in understanding the culture of this clinic and your journey here."

Jason leaned back in his chair and began to relax. "I'm happy to share, Professor. This clinic is a special place. It's more than just a workplace, it's a community and a haven."

John nodded, encouraging Jason to elaborate, "How so?"

"Well," Jason started, "here, I can be myself. I don't need a facade. Everyone here from the doctors to the administrative staff is open and accepting. We can be honest and vulnerable without fear of judgment. That is rare in today's world."

John scribbled notes excitedly, intrigued by Jason's words. "Can you give me an example of this openness?"

Jason's eyes softened and grew moist as he reflected on his past. "Absolutely. Dr. Henry Tuttle is a big part of why this place is so special. When I was younger, I had a lot of difficulties at home. My parents were going through a messy divorce and I was struggling to keep myself together. I used to come to the clinic for my regular check-ups, and Dr. Tuttle noticed something was off."

John leaned forward, sensing a significant story unfolding. "What did he do?"

"He listened," Jason said simply. "He asked me how I was doing—not just physically, but emotionally. And when I finally opened up to him about what was happening at home, he didn't judge. He just listened and offered his support. He became a refuge for me, a place where I could express my fears and anxieties without being dismissed or ridiculed."

"That must have been incredibly impactful," John remarked, his pen pausing on the page.

"It was," Jason confirmed. "Dr. Tuttle guided me through some of the toughest times in my life. He encouraged me to find healthy outlets for my stress and to focus on my education. His support inspired me to pursue a career in healthcare. I wanted to demonstrate that kind of

Family

support for others—to provide the same safe space that he provided for me."

John could see the deep gratitude in Jason's eyes. "And now you're here, continuing that legacy."

"Yes," Jason agreed, smiling in return. "Working here, I get to make a difference in people's lives every day. I try to be as understanding and supportive to our patients as Dr. Tuttle was to me. It's about creating a culture of trust and compassion, where people feel seen and heard."

John felt a surge of admiration for Jason and the work being done at the clinic. "How do you think this culture affects the patients?"

"I think it makes a world of difference," Jason said thoughtfully. "Patients feel more comfortable sharing their concerns and following through with treatments because they know we genuinely care about them. It leads to better health outcomes and a stronger community overall."

"Let me tell you one more story," Jason added. "Have you seen the signs on the reception desk and in the offices that say, "Remember Betty"?

"Yes, actually, I have," said John. "I wondered what they were about and meant to ask."

Jason went on to tell the story. "Several years ago, there was an office manager named Marissa Martinez. She was known throughout the office as the embodiment of patience and kindness. One of her tasks was to collect past-due bills. A patient named Betty Harper would come in every month for treatment. Every month she was late paying her bill, and every month, Marissa would call Betty to discuss her overdue payment. Each call followed a familiar pattern, an apology from Betty, an explanation that funds were tight and a request for an extension. Initially, Marissa found it perplexing how someone could be consistently behind on her bill, but over time, her interactions with Betty became less about the payments and more about the connection they shared.

Family

"'Hello, Mrs. Harper! It's Marissa from the clinic. How are you today?' Marissa would always start with genuine warmth.

"'Oh, Marissa, dear. It's lovely to hear your voice. I'm doing well, thank you. How are you?' Betty's voice, though frail, carried a softness that made Marissa smile.

"These calls, which began with the mundane task of arranging payment, soon blossomed into heartfelt conversations. Betty would share snippets of her life, stories from her past, and little anecdotes about her late husband. Marissa listened with rapt attention, her heart going out to the elderly woman who seemed to cherish these monthly interactions.

"As time went on, these calls grew longer, and she often set aside extra time to chat beyond the scope of business. Though she never fully understood why Betty couldn't pay her bill on time, Marissa didn't press too hard. She sensed that there was more to Betty's story; something unspoken that tied her to these calls.

"One day, Marissa made her usual call to Betty but there was no answer. Concerned, she tried several more times, but there was no answer. Days turned into weeks, and Marissa began to worry. She missed the warmth of her exchanges with Betty, the stories, hearing her gentle laughter.

"Several weeks later a letter arrived at the clinic, addressed to Marissa Martinez. The handwriting was delicate but shaky, immediately recognizable as Betty's. With trembling hands, Marissa opened the envelope and began to read:

Dear Marissa,

If you are reading this, it means I have passed on. I wanted to leave you a note to express my deepest gratitude for your kindness over these past few years. You see, I could have paid my bill on time; my finances were always secure. But after my husband passed away, I found myself alone and adrift. Our children live far away, and my days became long and lonely.

Your monthly calls became a beacon of light in my life—something to look forward to. You showed me compassion and

Family

kindness, not just as a customer service representative but as a friend. You listened to my stories, laughed at my jokes and made me feel valued and cared for. You made my last few years so much brighter, and for that, I am eternally grateful.

We never truly know the impact we have on others, but I wanted you to know that you made a profound difference in my life. Thank you, Marissa, for everything.

With love and gratitude,

Betty Harper

"That is the reason the words 'Remember Betty' are on every desk. It is a reminder not to judge; that when we create a safe environment for people to be honest and vulnerable, we are able to change lives."

John finished his notes and looked up, feeling inspired. "Thank you, Jason. Your story and the culture of this clinic are truly remarkable. It's clear that, with this clinic, Dr. Tuttle has created a lasting legacy."

Jason's eyes shone with pride. "I'm just grateful to be a part of it and to continue his work. It's an honor to help others the way he helped me."

As John finished his notes, he couldn't help but reflect on the profound impact one person can have on another's life. The haven that Dr. Tuttle had created for Jason was now being extended to countless others through the culture of the clinic. It was a testament to the power of empathy, support and genuine human connection.

At the bottom of his page he wrote and underlined the words: "Honesty and Vulnerability *without* judgment," and then added another circle to his diagram.

Family

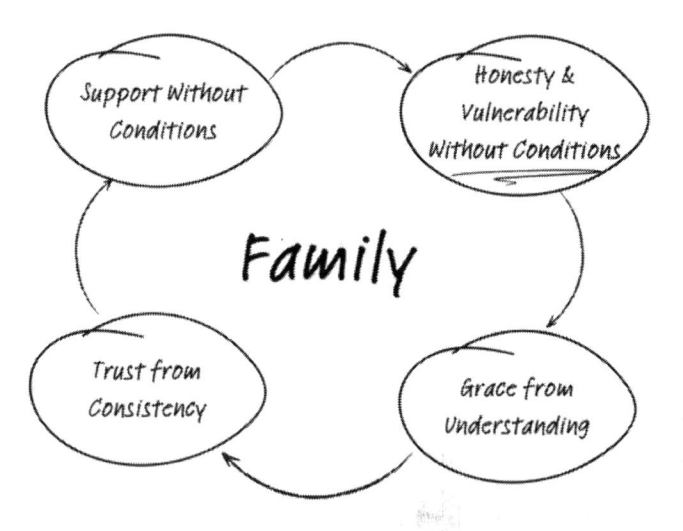

```
   Support Without              Honesty &
    Conditions                 Vulnerability
                             Without Conditions

                    Family

   Trust from                   Grace from
   Consistency                 Understanding
```

The picture was coming more into focus with every conversation.

Kent Myers

Family

11

Accountability with Forgiveness

John knew that there were only a couple more staff members left to complete all the interviews. Over the past 48 hours, he'd had the opportunity to gain a degree of clarity about the culture that Henry was so careful to protect. The more he understood it, the more he admired what had been built there. He was particularly eager to speak with Nurse Roger Adams, a veteran staff member renowned for his wisdom and compassionate approach to nursing.

John glanced up as Roger entered the room, his presence exuding a calm confidence that immediately put others at ease. They exchanged greetings and, after a few minutes of small talk, settled into the conversation.

"Roger, I'm sure you have heard the stories of why I'm here. I have had the opportunity to talk to just about all of the staff at this point and am trying to get a clear understanding of the culture here and specifically the aspects of the culture that need to be preserved during the leadership transition. Can you tell me more about what the culture here means to you and how it plays out in your daily work?" John began, his curiosity palpable.

Roger smiled thoughtfully, leaning back in his chair. "This is a wonderful place. You see, I grew up on the East Coast and was accustomed to straight talk, no candy-coating difficult conversations. Sometimes it is hard to deal with 'Midwestern nice' where passive-aggressive behavior runs rampant. One of the things that I appreciate the most is the fact that we trust each other so much that we have created a culture of 'Accountability with Forgiveness' where we can give each other honest feedback and hold one another accountable, but without holding grudges. It's a delicate but essential balance."

He paused for a moment, collecting his thoughts before continuing, "Let me give you a few examples. Just last week one of our newer nurses made a medication error. It was a stressful situation, but instead of berating her, we sat down and discussed what happened. We reviewed the protocols and identified where things went wrong. She understood her mistake, and we took steps to ensure it wouldn't happen again. But the *key* part was what happened afterward."

Roger's expression softened as he leaned forward. "We forgave her. We didn't dwell on the mistake or let it define her. She learned from it, and we moved on. Holding a grudge wouldn't have helped anyone – it would only have created a toxic atmosphere and hindered her growth. Forgiveness in this context freed both her and us from carrying that burden."

John nodded, intrigued. "And how does that affect the team and cultural dynamics?"

"Clearly it builds trust," Roger replied without hesitation. "When people know they won't be unfairly judged or punished for their mistakes, they're more open to learning and improving. They don't have to walk on eggshells. It fosters a sense of safety and mutual respect. Of course, this doesn't mean we ignore mistakes or let things slide; accountability is crucial. But it's about handling those moments constructively from a perspective of caring, not criticizing."

He continued with another example, this one more personal. "A few years ago, I had a disagreement with a colleague over patient care. It got heated and I said some things I regretted. The next day, I approached him and apologized. He could have held onto that anger, but he chose to forgive me. We talked it out, understood each other's perspectives, and moved forward. That experience strengthened our professional relationship rather than

Family

damaging it."

John scribbled notes furiously, captivated by the practical wisdom Roger was sharing. "How does forgiveness impact you personally, Roger?"

Roger's eyes softened as he spoke. "Forgiveness has a powerful impact on the one who forgives. Carrying a grudge is like carrying a heavy load—it weighs you down and affects your well-being. When you forgive, you let go of that burden. It's liberating. It allows you to focus on the present and future rather than being stuck in the past."

John paused, reflecting on Roger's words. "It sounds like forgiveness requires a lot of strength."

"It does," Roger agreed. "It's not always easy, especially when the hurt runs deep. But it's a choice—a choice to prioritize healing and growth over resentment. And in a healthcare setting, where emotions and stakes are high, this approach is invaluable. It keeps us focused on our mission: providing the best care for our patients."

The room fell silent for a moment as John absorbed the profound implications of Roger's insights. The idea of blending accountability with forgiveness seemed both simple and revolutionary, offering a path to a healthier, more resilient work environment.

"Thank you, Roger," John finally said, his voice filled with genuine appreciation. "Your perspective is enlightening. I can see why you think this clinic is such a wonderful place."

Roger smiled warmly. "I'm glad to share. It's a team effort, and we all play a part in maintaining this culture. If we can help each other grow while extending grace, we're not just better healthcare providers, we become better people."

As Roger left the office John sat back in his chair, contemplating the lessons he had learned. The concept of "Accountability with Forgiveness" resonated deeply with him, promising not only a blueprint for professional conduct but also a powerful philosophy for life. He knew that this principle would be a pivotal part of his ongoing study and would offer valuable insights into the heart of the clinic's success.

Family

John stared deeply into his empty coffee cup while he flipped the page of his notebook. At the end of his notes from his interview with Roger, he wrote the words "Accountability with Forgiveness" and underlined it twice.

John then added another circle to his simple but meaningful diagram.

Family diagram with five circles around the word "Family": Honesty & Vulnerability Without Conditions, Accountability with Forgiveness, Grace from Understanding, Trust from Consistency, Support Without Conditions.

John placed both hands around his empty coffee cup with two things on his mind. First, he thought about how beneficial it would have been to hear Roger's wisdom earlier in his life and how many burdens of grudges and hard feelings he carried for far too long. Secondly, he thought—with a sense of confidence—that he was ready to conquer the evil coffee machine to get another cup of coffee. As John headed toward the breakroom, he glanced down at his watch. He couldn't believe that the morning was gone, so instead of another cup of coffee he decided that he would treat himself to lunch at Molly's café.

As he exited his office, he was looking down and he almost ran smack into Victoria, the clinic administrator. "I am so sorry, Victoria. I wasn't looking where I was going. My apologies." Victoria was a retired Army nurse. Her colleagues often described her as the "glue that holds the clinic together."

"No problem, Professor. Actually, I was just coming to see you. I believe I may be your last interview. I hope they have all gone well and are providing some insight into the people of the clinic."

Family

John, with a smile on his face, said, "Very insightful. It is clear that the people create the culture, and the culture has created the best within the people. I really look forward to spending some time with you, but I was just on my way to Molly's for some lunch. Could we catch up early this afternoon?"

"Of course, Professor," Victoria replied. "I will be in my office all afternoon. Just poke your head back in when you get back. Also, tell Molly I said, 'Hello.'"

John thought to himself, *I love the sense of community in a small town.* "Sure I will, see you this afternoon," he said as he walked down the hallway toward the clinic door.

12

Lunch Time

The clinic's sunlit corridors which were bustling with patients and staff now felt oddly quiet as he made his way to the exit. He glanced at his watch—12:30 p.m.—just in time for lunch. Stepping outside, he was greeted by the familiar sights and sounds of Main Street. The summer sun cast a warm glow over the quaint town, where flower boxes burst with color and shop owners greeted passersby with friendly waves.

Family

John took a leisurely stroll down the street, his mind still churning through the morning's conversations. As he thought back on it all, he realized what a blessing it was that his old friend Henry had asked for help, bringing him back to his hometown. After all the decades, this street and this town still seemed much the same: warm, welcoming, and friendly. He realized that that sentiment was like the stories he'd been hearing all morning. The recurring theme he heard from nearly every staff member was intriguing: a profound sense of family and community.

He arrived at Molly's Café, a local favorite with its cheerful blue awning and the irresistible scent of fresh bread wafting out the door. As he entered, he was met with a chorus of greetings. Molly,waved him over to his usual spot—a cozy corner booth by the window.

"Hey there, Professor Hill!" she called out, a broad smile lighting up her face. "I'll be right with you."

John settled into the booth, ensconced in the familiar comfort of the café. The daily specials were written on a chalkboard, and Molly's voice soon followed to announce them with enthusiasm. "Today we've got chicken pot pie, veggie lasagna and the best meatloaf you've ever tasted!"

"I'll go with the meatloaf," John decided. Molly nodded, making a note on her pad before heading back to the kitchen.

The café hummed with activity, but it wasn't long before Molly herself returned, this time without her order pad. She slid into the seat across from John, her expression curious. "How are those interviews coming along?" she asked, leaning forward slightly.

John took a sip of his water and smiled. "They're going well, actually. I keep hearing about this strong sense of community here. Everyone talks about the clinic like it's more than just a place of work. It's like a family."

Molly nodded knowingly. "That's exactly what it is. You know, last Friday night, there was a baseball game. The clinic staff were all there, even Dr. Sara. They sat together, laughed together, cheered for the same team. It wasn't just about watching the game. They were bonding, supporting each other, just like they do at work. It's a special thing to witness."

John listened intently, absorbing her words. "That's incredible. It's rare to see such camaraderie in a workplace. It definitely explains the high morale and dedication I've been noticing."

Molly smiled warmly. "They're more than coworkers; they're friends who get to work together. And that's reflected in the care they provide. Patients feel it, too. It's like being taken care of by family."

As she spoke, John's meal arrived—steaming hot meatloaf with a side of mashed potatoes and green beans. The aroma made his stomach growl. He thanked Molly and began to eat, savoring the hearty, comforting flavors.

They chatted a bit more, Molly sharing stories about the clinic staff and their various escapades. John felt that he now had a deeper understanding and appreciation for the unique environment at the clinic.

After finishing his lunch, he thanked Molly and paid his bill, promising to return soon. He was barely out of the door before he heard:

"John Hill! Is that you?"

He turned to see Julie Miller, the florist from the shop next to the café, stepping out of her store with a bright smile on her face and a few loose petals clinging to her apron. Julie was a well-known figure in the small town. Her warm personality was as colorful as the flowers she tended.

"Julie, hi! How are you?" John greeted her with a genuine smile, momentarily forgetting his worries.

"I'm good, busy as always. You know how it is with flowers—there's always something needing a bit of extra care," she said, laughing lightly. "I've been meaning to catch you. I heard you're helping out at the clinic during the transition."

"That's right," John replied, his smile fading slightly. "It's been quite an adjustment for everyone involved."

Family

Julie nodded understandingly. "I can imagine. Change is never easy. But I wanted to share a story with you—something that might lift your spirits a bit."

Intrigued, John stopped walking and turned to face her fully. Julie began recounting her story as they walked slowly down the street.

"A few years back, my son Tommy had a nasty fall while playing in the yard. He hit his head pretty hard, and I was beside myself with worry. Dr. Henry was out for a walk that afternoon and happened to pass by our house. When he heard what had happened, he insisted on coming in to take a look at Tommy."

John listened intently as Julie spoke, her voice filled with emotion.

"Dr. Henry was so kind and calm. He examined Tommy right there in our living room, assuring me every step of the way. Thankfully, it wasn't anything serious, just a bump and a scare. But what really stuck with me was his genuine concern. In a time when everything seems to be about money, it was heartening to see a doctor who saw the humanity in his patients before anything else."

John could see the sincerity in Julie's eyes as she continued. "Dr. Henry didn't ask for any payment or make it about the bottom line. He was just there, caring for my son because that's what he felt was right. It's a kind of compassion that's rare these days." Julie paused, her eyes misting slightly. "I think that's what makes our clinic special, John. It's not just about the services we provide, but the way we provide them. People feel cared for, respected, and valued. That's a legacy Dr. Tuttle started, and I know it's something Sara can continue."

John felt a wave of emotion wash over him. The pressure of the clinic's transition had been weighing heavily on him, and Julie's story was an additional understanding of what Henry is trying to protect. He reached out and squeezed Julie's hand. "Thank you, Julie. Your story means a lot. We all get caught up in the challenges and forget the bigger picture. But hearing this reminds me of why this clinic exists."

Family

Julie smiled warmly. "I thought it might help. The community trusts Sara. They know she cares, just like her father. She'll do great things at the clinic, I'm sure of it."

As they parted ways, John started back on his path to the clinic. The walk back felt shorter, his mind now focused on his final interview of the day with Victoria, the clinic administrator. He was eager to hear her perspective, knowing it would provide the last piece of the puzzle.

Upon entering the clinic he made his way to Victoria's office. The air was filled with a sense of purpose and the hum of activity. John knocked on the door, and Victoria's voice called out for him to enter.

"Professor Hill, how was lunch?" she asked, greeting him with a professional yet friendly smile. "Ready to wrap up our conversation?"

"Absolutely," John replied, "take your time. I will be back in the office when you are ready."

John continued down the corridor, and as he turned the corner into the small office, he thought that this would be a significant afternoon as it was the last interview in this process of discovery for his friend. Victoria had been a very loyal and instrumental team member, so he was excited to hear her insights and perspective on the transition.

Family

13

Build Each Other Up

Victoria entered the office with her usual warm smile, carrying a small notebook and a cup of tea. She had been with the clinic for over two decades and had seen it evolve in countless ways. As she took a seat opposite Professor Hill, the room felt charged with a sense of reflection and anticipation.

"Victoria," John began, his voice steady but tinged with nostalgia. "I've been looking forward to this

Family

conversation. You've been such an integral part of the clinic's success. I'd love to hear your thoughts on what has made this place special."

Victoria nodded thoughtfully. "Thank you, Professor Hill. It's been an incredible journey. One of the key aspects that has made our clinic stand out is the way our staff members build each other up. This place isn't just about providing excellent medical care; it's about creating a supportive community."

She paused, gathering her thoughts. "You know, in my role, I've had the privilege of observing and fostering this culture. I've seen how recognition and appreciation play distinct yet complementary roles here. Recognition is about acknowledging achievements and milestones. It's important, but it can sometimes feel formal and structured. Appreciation, on the other hand, is more personal and spontaneous. It's about valuing people for who they are and for the unique qualities they bring to our team."

John leaned in, his interest piqued. "Can you share some stories that illustrate this difference?"

"Absolutely," Victoria replied, her eyes lighting up. "I remember a nurse, Hannah, who went above and beyond during a particularly hectic flu season. She received formal recognition through an award—which was well-deserved—but what really moved her was the appreciation she received from her colleagues. Small notes left in her locker, a surprise coffee run organized by the team and heartfelt words of gratitude during meetings. These acts of appreciation made her feel truly valued and supported."

Victoria continued, "Another example is our janitor, Mr. Hernandez. He's one of the unsung heroes of our clinic. His dedication and hard work often go unnoticed in formal settings. But the staff make it a point to appreciate him daily with a simple 'thank you,' a smile or a shared lunch break. It's these little gestures that build a sense of belonging and significance."

Professor Hill nodded, deeply moved by the stories. "It's clear that you've created an environment where people feel seen and valued. How do you think this impacts the overall quality of life in the clinic?"

Family

Victoria's expression grew serious. "We spend around 90,000 hours of our lives working. During our working lives, we often spend more of our waking hours with our colleagues than we do with our families. The relationships we build at work and the way we support each other profoundly impact our quality of life. When we build each other up, we create a positive environment that benefits everyone. It's not just about getting the job done, it's about ensuring that everyone feels like they matter, that they're making a meaningful impact."

She leaned forward, her voice soft but resolute. "Every person in the world wants to feel valuable, and to know that they are making an impact. When we build each other up, we fulfill this fundamental human need. We create a culture where everyone feels empowered and appreciated, which in turn improves our work and the care we provide to our patients."

John took a deep breath, feeling the weight of her words. "It sounds like the clinic is more than just a workplace, it's a community where people thrive."

Victoria smiled. "Exactly. By practicing both recognition and appreciation, we've created a great quality of life for everyone here. It's a place where people look forward to coming to work because they know they're valued and that they're making a difference. But that isn't all," Victoria paused.

John raised an eyebrow, intrigued. "What else?"

"Positive gossip," Victoria said simply. Seeing his puzzled expression, she continued. "You see, in many places, gossip has a negative connotation. It's associated with spreading rumors and creating divisions. But here, we've turned it on its head. Everyone in the clinic talks well about each other when they aren't around. We build each other up, share each other's accomplishments and highlight our strengths. It creates a culture of mutual respect and admiration. For example, when someone mentions how well Dr. Sara handled a tricky diagnosis, it's shared with others, and the respect for her skill grows. Or when the nurses talk about how patient and kind Roger is with the more anxious patients, it boosts morale and sets a positive example."

Family

John nodded slowly, beginning to grasp the concept. "That sounds... really uplifting. But how do you ensure it doesn't turn into just empty flattery?"

"Good question," Victoria replied, appreciating his insight. "We focus on genuine praise. It's not about making things up or exaggerating, it's about recognizing and acknowledging the real strengths and efforts of our colleagues. And because it's genuine, it builds trust and a sense of unity. It is not a 'participation' award."

She paused, letting that sink in before continuing. "There's also something we call the 'Mom versus Dad' syndrome. It's when—in many settings—one person might say 'no,' and then you go to another authority figure hoping for a 'yes.' It's a common issue, especially in clinics where multiple supervisors or senior staff are involved. But here, Dr. Henry and I have managed to avoid that problem by presenting a united front. Over the years, Dr. Henry and I have made it a point to always talk well about each other when the other isn't around. We build each other up in front of the staff. If someone comes to me with an issue, they know that Dr. Henry and I are on the same page because they've heard me praising his decisions and judgment when he's not there, and vice versa. It reinforces our solidarity and prevents any attempt to play one of us against the other."

John smiled, clearly impressed. "That sounds like a really healthy work environment. It must make a huge difference in how the clinic operates."

"It does," Victoria agreed. "It creates an atmosphere of trust and respect. When the staff sees that we, the leaders, respect and trust each other, they follow suit. It trickles down. And it's not just about Dr. Henry and me, the entire team sees the value in this approach. It's part of our culture now."

She leaned forward, her eyes sparkling with enthusiasm. "John, positive gossip isn't just about being nice. It's about creating a foundation of mutual respect and admiration that holds everything together. It's about recognizing that everyone has something valuable to contribute and making sure that everyone knows their contributions are appreciated."

Family

John nodded, clearly inspired. "I see what you mean. It's a simple concept, but it makes a huge impact."

"Exactly," Victoria said, her smile warm, "and it's something I hope to carry forward with Dr. Sara. Building each other up when we're not around isn't just good for morale, it's essential for a cohesive, efficient and happy clinic."

As the interview concluded, Professor Hill felt a profound sense of satisfaction. Victoria had encapsulated the essence of what made the clinic special. It wasn't just the medical care or the professional achievements, it was the genuine human connections and the culture of mutual support and appreciation that truly set it apart. It truly is like a family.

As John wrapped up his notes, he reached the bottom of the page where, in all capitals, he wrote and underlined the phrase "**BUILD EACH OTHER UP!!**" with two exclamation marks. He then flipped a few pages back to the simple diagram he had been creating and added a new circle to the picture:

```
        Honesty &                 Accountability with
       Vulnerability                  Forgiveness
     Without Conditions

   Support Without                     Build Each
      Conditions         Family         Other Up!!

        Trust from                    Grace from
        Consistency                  Understanding
```

John felt that this picture had come fully into focus. Now John completely understood why Henry had called him there and what he was working to protect, and it was time for the big challenge. How did he consolidate all this information and communicate it to everyone?

Family

John didn't know the answer, but he knew where he would go to find them—the same place where he would go while growing up to contemplate life and think: the dugout at the ballpark. This was a place filled with some of the best memories of his childhood and the times he and Henry spent as friends and teammates.

Kent Myers

Family

14

The Dugout

Professor Hill walked slowly along the worn path leading to the old baseball field, his steps deliberate. The sun was beginning to set, casting a warm, golden glow over the ballpark he had once called home. The air was thick with the scent of summer and the sound of children laughing in the distance, which brought back memories of days long past. As he approached the field, the familiar sight of the dugout came into view. It was exactly as he remembered it—a simple structure of weathered wood—yet it held for him a profound significance.

The dugout had been a sanctuary for John and his best friend, Dr. Henry Tuttle, during their childhood. It was here that they had spent countless hours playing baseball, sharing dreams and contemplating the mysteries of life. Today, it was a place of reflection for John; a place to process the whirlwind of emotions and revelations from the past two days.

He took a seat on the splintered bench, the wood creaking under his weight as he let out a deep sigh. The interviews with the clinic staff had been revealing, intense and, at times, overwhelming. Every person he spoke to had painted a vivid picture of the culture Henry had painstakingly nurtured over the last forty years. It was a culture that everyone described as "family," a word that carried a depth of meaning.

He opened his notebook and stared at the simple diagram he had sketched on the last page.

Family

- Honesty & Vulnerability Without Conditions
- Accountability with Forgiveness
- Support Without Conditions
- **Family**
- Build Each Other Up!!
- Trust from Consistency
- Grace from Understanding

John closed his eyes, recalling the voices of the people he had met. There was Roger, the nurse who had been with the clinic for many years and whose eyes were filled with warmth as he spoke about "accountability with forgiveness." He had told John about the times he had made mistakes and how Henry had held him accountable, but always with an underlying grace.

Then there was Emily, the receptionist whose dedication to the clinic went beyond her job description. She had shared stories of how the staff always had each other's back, no matter the circumstances. "Unconditionally," she had emphasized. "It's not just a word here; it's a way of life."

John remembered Jason, a young MA whom he had known as a young boy and who was now a grown man working in the clinic. He had talked about the freedom to be honest and vulnerable without fear of judgment. "It's rare," he had admitted, "but here, we can be ourselves, flaws and all." He remembered the story Jason had shared about the kind letter from the patient after her passing; "Remember Betty."

He thought of Judy, the nurse, whose kindness seemed to permeate the very walls of the clinic. She had spoken about the grace that came from understanding each other deeply. "We trust each other's consistency," she had said, "and that trust extends to the way we serve our patients."

The dugout seemed to breathe with the echoes of these voices, each one reinforcing the other. John opened his eyes and looked out over the empty field, now bathed in the soft, amber light of the setting sun. This place, much like the

Family

clinic, had a soul. It was a testament to the enduring power of connection, compassion and community.

As kids, this dugout had been where he and Henry had laid the foundations of their friendship—dreaming of bright and boundless futures. Now, it was a place for John to reconcile the past with the present; to understand the legacy Henry had built. It was clear that Henry's vision had transcended the confines of the clinic walls. It was alive in the hearts of all members of the staff, manifested in their actions, their interactions and in the way they treated each other and their patients.

John took a deep breath, feeling a sense of clarity. The culture Henry had created was more than just a professional environment, it was a living, breathing entity that thrived on the principles of empathy, trust and unconditional support. It was a family, bound not by blood, but by a shared commitment to something greater than themselves.

As John sat in the dugout, the memories of his childhood came flooding back to him. He remembered his high school baseball coach, and in his mind, the words "*hold the rope*" resonated against the concrete walls of the dugout. His high school baseball coach was a significant influence on his life.

Every season, Coach Gambel would sit down with each new freshman player. He would take time to set expectations, share values and instill in him the beliefs of the team. When he ended his little pep talk, he would hand him a small piece of rope and tell him, "On this team, every day you will hear: *'hold the rope.'*"

He then went on to explain.

"Imagine that you are hanging from the edge of a cliff 20,000 feet high. The only thing between you and a fall to certain death is a rope with the person(s) of your choice holding on to the other end. Who would you trust to hold the rope so you could climb to safety? Who would let the rope scar their hands and still refuse to let go? How many people could you count on who would withstand burning pain, and watch blood drip from their hands for you?

Family

"When you get to the first practice, look around and ask yourself, 'Who could I trust to hold the rope? Who could I count on to overcome the pain for me?' When you can look at every member on this team and say to yourself, 'They would *all* hold the rope,' then we are destined to be champions. You see, the team that holds the rope when the going gets tough… wins. When the last inning of a game arrives and the score is close and fatigue and pain have set in, tell your teammates, 'I'll hold the rope, I'll overcome the pain and hold the rope for you,' then ask them to hold it for you."

As John recalled those words, he realized that the words of a coach decades ago influenced Henry and the culture he created in the clinic. That thought became almost overwhelming as he considered the hidden impact we have in the words we say. Words are very powerful.

As the last rays of sunlight dipped below the horizon, John felt a renewed sense of purpose and clarity. He knew that his task was not just to preserve Henry's legacy, but to ensure that it continued to grow and evolve. The dugout, once a place of childhood dreams, had now become a symbol of the future he was determined to protect.

With a final look around, John stood up and began to walk back, his steps lighter than before. He carried with him the wisdom of the past and a hope for the future, ready to embrace the challenges ahead. The field behind him grew quiet, but in his heart, the echoes of the dugout's lessons would always remain.

He knew the task ahead of him was to pull everyone together and to talk about the lessons he had heard and then determine the direction ahead.

Family

15

The Report

John had a restless night's sleep, wondering how the meeting in the morning would go and how all the insights he had gathered would be received by Henry and Sara. As the morning came and he entered the conference room the sun was streaming through the large windows, casting a warm glow over the polished table. John came in and slowly sat down in one of the large leather chairs directly across the table from Henry and Sara.

Family

Henry's face was a mix of pride and apprehension as he looked at Sara, who radiated a quiet confidence. The room was filled with the aroma of freshly brewed coffee, setting a comfortable tone for the important discussion ahead.

"Good morning, John," Henry began, breaking the silence. "We're eager to hear what you've gathered from your interviews with the staff."

John nodded, opening his leather-bound notebook. "Good morning, Henry, Sara. Over the past couple of days I've had the opportunity to speak with almost everyone at the clinic. Let me start with this: this clinic is a rare place. It is a place where people feel heard and respected, a place where they all look forward to coming to work every day. I understand your feelings of protectiveness. What stood out the most was the recurring mention of the word 'family.'" He paused, letting the weight of the word sink in. "It's written on the break room wall, and it's more than just a word here. It's the essence of what this place represents to everyone who works at the clinic."

Henry leaned forward, his eyes sparkling with interest. "Family, yes. That's exactly what I hoped you'd find."

John reached into his bag and pulled out a diagram, carefully placing it on the table. "I've distilled the concept of 'family' into six perspectives based on my conversations." He pointed to the first segment. "Trust from the consistency of our attitudes and behaviors."

Family diagram with six surrounding bubbles: Honesty & Vulnerability Without Conditions; Accountability with Forgiveness; Build Each Other Up!!; Grace from Understanding; Trust from Consistency; Support Without Conditions.

He continued around the circle. "Support without Conditions, we always have each other's back. Giving each other grace because we know each other beyond the job title and role we play. The ability to be honest and vulnerable with each other and not be judged."

Family

John paused before the final two segments. "Accountability, but with forgiveness and without holding grudges. And lastly, building each other up every day in the words we say and the gratitude and appreciation we show one another."

Henry's eyes widened as he looked at the diagram. "That is it… that defines the culture that I want to ensure lives through this transition of leadership to Sara."

Sara, who had been listening intently, felt a new understanding dawn upon her. For the first time, she truly grasped what her father wanted to protect. She looked at Henry and said with her voice soft but firm, "Of course I commit to continue fostering this culture. We are a family—I learned that from you, Dad, not from medical school."

Henry smiled, a mix of relief and pride washing over him. "I know you will continue what I started, Sara. This place means so much to everyone, and I'm confident you'll honor that legacy. The change people fear is not technology, policies, or procedures, but the relationships we have from the culture we promote."

John leaned back, satisfied with the response. "The next step is to communicate this to the staff and engage them in how we move forward. It's crucial to create stability, confidence, ownership and optimism for the future."

Sara nodded. "I agree. We should have an all-staff meeting to discuss the direction and to gain their insights. It's important to be intentional about the words we use, the attitudes we have, and the behaviors we exemplify every day."

Henry added, "We need to ensure that everyone feels they are part of this journey. Their voices matter, and their contributions are what make this place a family."

John stood up, gathering his notes. "Let's plan the meeting for the end of the day. It will be like how things used to be. We will order pizza and just sit and have a conversation. We will talk *with* them and not *at* them."

Family

Sara smiled, feeling a sense of clarity and purpose. "Thank you, John. And Dad, thank you for trusting me with this. Together, we'll make sure this clinic continues to be a place where family is at the heart of everything we do."

The meeting concluded with a renewed sense of unity and direction. As they left the conference room, the morning sun seemed a little brighter, promising a future built on the strong foundation of family. There was still much work to be done before the meeting at the end of the day. John headed back to his office to start working on the game plan.

Kent Myers

16

Building the Common Language

John Hill had been meticulously planning this meeting all day. The weight of its significance hung heavy on his mind as he gathered his thoughts and refined his notes. As the day unfolded he went over his presentation again and again, ensuring that every word carried the impact he intended. By late afternoon, it was time.

John called everyone into the conference room: Dr. Henry Hill and Dr. Sara Hill, his trusted colleagues and partners in the clinic; Emily, the ever-cheerful receptionist who was often the first point of contact for patients; Victoria, the clinic administrator whose meticulous organization kept everything running smoothly; Nurse Judy Walters and Nurse Jason, whose skills and compassionate care were the backbone of the clinic; and Roger, the diligent medical assistant who always went the extra mile.

As they settled into their seats, a quiet buzz of curiosity filled the room. John stood at the head of the table, taking a moment to make eye contact with each person. He drew a deep breath, feeling the gravity of the moment.

"Thank you all for coming," John began, his voice steady and clear. "I've had the opportunity to speak with each of you over the past couple of days, and those conversations have confirmed something I always believed: What makes our clinic special is the sense of family we've built here."

Family

He paused, letting his words sink in. He saw nods of agreement and felt the shared sense of pride.

"Today," John continued, "I want to talk about how we can sustain this culture and how we can ensure it becomes and remains the very fabric of our daily lives. This isn't just about a mission statement or a set of values written on a wall, it needs to be lived out every day in our attitudes, in our behaviors and most importantly, in the words we use."

John moved to a whiteboard at the front of the room where he had drawn a simple diagram. At the center was the word, "Family." He spent the next several minutes walking through all the stories he heard and the six pillars that explained, defined and articulated the meaning of this word: vulnerability without judgment, accountability with forgiveness, support without conditions, trust from consistency, grace from understanding and building each other up every day.

John paused for a moment after his explanation, looked down at the floor, and then lifted his head and said,

"This word and these explanations surprised and confused me." Everyone stared at Professor Hill in astonishment.

John went on to say that he had this word backward, "In my career in academia, we have been told that there is no place for *family* in work. We are told that family means we must all

Family diagram with surrounding concepts: Honesty & Vulnerability Without Conditions, Accountability with Forgiveness, Build Each Other Up!!, Grace from Understanding, Trust from Consistency, Support Without Conditions

think exactly alike and share everything—that we behave unprofessionally, that we have no boundaries in our relationships. Some may also believe that we surrender all work-life balance if we are like a family, or that we may be

Family

scared of close relationships/friendships with co-workers in a day of layoffs and downsizing."

"And now how do you see that word?" Henry asked.

"*No longer* as something that means *dysfunction* and *division*, but rather *team* and *unity*," John replied. He turned back toward the whiteboard. "This," John said, pointing to the word FAMILY, "is the core of who you are. But to keep this culture thriving, it needs to be more than a concept. It needs to be part of our daily vocabulary. The words we use with each other and with our patients are powerful. They shape our environment and our interactions."

He turned back to the group, the intensity of his conviction shining in his eyes. "I want us to create a shared vocabulary that embodies our culture of Family; words and phrases that remind us of who we are and how we treat each other. Something simple but profound that we can use every day."

John handed out small slips of paper and pens to everyone. "Take a few minutes to think about this. What phrase or few words can become part of our vocabulary to protect and nurture this culture? Write down whatever comes to mind."

The room fell into a thoughtful silence as everyone considered John's request. John watched as they wrote, feeling a sense of anticipation. He knew this exercise was more than just symbolic, it was a tangible step toward strengthening their shared values.

After a few minutes, John collected the slips of paper. He was eager to see the responses and read them aloud, one by one.

John slowly unfolded each piece of paper and revealed each response. As he did, a smile came across his face. On one of them, he saw a familiar response and immediately knew who the author was. It said, in capital letters: *HOLD THE ROPE.*

Just 24 hours earlier he'd had the same thoughts and reminisced on the same memories of a coach who'd influenced his life and Henry's.

Family

John held up the small piece of paper and said, "I am not psychic, but I know who wrote this one: 'HOLD THE ROPE.' Anyone want to claim and explain this one?"

Henry sheepishly smiled and raised his hand. "I thought you might recognize that phrase, John," Henry said. Henry went on to tell the story of Coach Gambel and his pep talk to incoming freshmen. "Those words followed by actions greatly influenced my life, and after 40 years, I still remember them as if I'd just heard them yesterday for the first time," Henry concluded.

As Henry finished, every head in the room was nodding in agreement. As John said this, he turned to the whiteboard and said, "Okay, here is the first phrase in our common language of culture."

On the board, he wrote the words:

HOLD THE ROPE

John turned back to the room and reached for another piece of paper.

Kent Myers

17

Give Trust

Professor Hill reached for another piece of paper. The atmosphere of the room had shifted from that of tension and anxiety to optimism and curiosity.

As John unfolded the paper he read the words, "GIVE TRUST." As he read them aloud Judy Walters, with a smile of nervous pride on her face, slowly raised her hand.

"Could you enlighten us on what those words mean to you, Judy?" asked John.

"I think trust is one of these things we get backward in our lives," Judy started. "What if we changed our perspective on trust and rather than seeing trust as a prize to be won, we see it instead as a gift that we bestow on others? So many have grown up believing that trust is earned. I believe we have that backward. Trust is not something that is earned by another, it is our decision whether to give it or not. **Trust can never be earned; it can only be GIVEN.** What if part of our vocabulary was 'GIVE TRUST?'"

Judy's voice began to fill with passion as she spoke those words. "This is a concept that may be completely backward to many of us. We may struggle with this concept because it places the responsibility on us as the *givers* of trust, versus the behaviors of the *earners* of trust.

"When we really think about it, we realize how unfair it is to wait on another to tell us that our trust has been earned. When we subscribe to this ideology, it means that we are, in effect, 'keeping score.' Every time we do so we create a

Family

winner and a loser, and in the game of relationships, everyone loses. When you wait for people to earn your trust, you are not sharing your scoring system. Nobody knows how to win and therefore they can't be expected to meet your unspoken needs. It is impossible to be good enough, long enough and consistent enough to keep in high standings. Everyone will fall short during their journey from time to time, and this journey has no end. Earning trust is 'me' and 'you' focused. The more I focus on me and what I need, want and desire in a relationship, the less room there is for me to give you what you need, want and desire. In essence, requiring others to earn your trust is a selfish act. Trust is not only your responsibility when you want it, but being able to trust others is your responsibility as well. In other words, if you are to have trust in your relationships, it starts and ends with you.

"I fully realize that this line of thinking might make you very uneasy. It's not for casual encounters, and it certainly doesn't mean that you should post your banking information on social media. This line of thinking is for the benefit and the legacy of the culture of this clinic where we have a high level of trust, and where winning the relationship game is key.

"When we change our perspective, we realize that trust is a choice—a choice that we control. **GIVE TRUST.**" The room was completely silent. Judy, a typically quiet and reserved nurse, spoke these words with passion and power that clearly moved the room.

As she sat back in her chair, John went to the board and said, "Well, tell us how you *really* feel, Judy." The tension broke with laughter and an admiration for Judy's passion. John turned to the whiteboard and wrote the words:

HOLD THE ROPE

GIVE TRUST

With the final stroke of the marker, the room erupted in applause. John could sense the momentum in the room as he reached for another piece of paper.

Family

Kent Myers

18

Progress Not Perfection

John approached the table and reached for another piece of paper; it was meticulously folded in perfect symmetry. As he opened the piece of paper and read the words, the irony became clear to him.

"Wow, this one might be tough for many of us… progress, not perfection."

Jason, the nurse—a new hire—looked up and raised his hand. "That one is mine," he said. "I don't want to be

Family

controversial, but I realize that I am not perfect. None of us is One of my earliest memories is drawing a picture of—something, I am not sure what it was supposed to be, but I remember the mistake that I made. My marker slipped and an inadvertent line appeared, ruining my drawing. My lip began to tremble. The picture has long since disappeared, but that feeling of deep frustration and shame has lingered.

"More often than I'd like to admit, something seemingly inconsequential will cause the same feeling to crop up again. Something as minor as sending an email with a spelling mistake or calling a patient by the wrong name can tumble around in my mind for days, accompanied by occasional discourteous voices admonishing me for my stupidity, telling me that I should have done better. I know this is baggage I carry, but I bet I am not alone." As Jason looked around the room, he could see heads nodding in support and understanding, and empathetic eyes looking back at him.

He continued, "In today's society, we often see perfection as a positive. Even admitting that you are a perfectionist can come off as coyly self-congratulating. At job interviews it's almost a clichéd response to the question, 'What's your worst trait?'

"I believe we focus too much on perfection because we fear things are not good enough. If we live in pursuit of perfection, we forever have the what-should-be mindset. The reality is that life is not perfect and even if we think *elements* of our lives are, what does it actually mean to be perfect? The definition is different for every individual, so achieving 'perfect' results is an impracticality that holds us back both professionally and personally."

He paused, scanning the room to make sure he had everyone's attention. "In the medical field, we often strive for perfection. While aiming high is admirable, it can also be incredibly stressful and, frankly, unrealistic. The constant pressure to be perfect can lead to burnout and dissatisfaction. It can even lead to a negative impact on both our mental health and the quality of care that we provide."

The staff nodded, many showing signs of agreement. Jason stood up and continued, "But what if we shift our focus from being perfect to simply making progress? Small,

Family

consistent improvements *every day* can lead to significant positive outcomes. This isn't about lowering standards, it's about recognizing that every step forward, no matter how small, is valuable."

He could see the wheels turning in their minds. "For instance, consider our patient interactions. Instead of getting frustrated because we couldn't solve all their problems in one visit, let's celebrate the progress we make with them. Maybe today we helped a patient better understand his condition. Maybe we assisted another patient in taking the first step towards a healthier lifestyle. These are all wins. **Progress, not perfection**."

With a conclusive deep breath, Jason sat back down.

John stepped forward and asked, "Progress, not perfection—should that be a part of our cultural vocabulary?"

The room erupted with a resounding, "Yes!" As people talked, Jason quickly realized he was not alone in his quest to stop pursuing perfection.

Kent Myers

"Well, that sounds unanimous to me," John said, as he walked toward the whiteboard and added to his list:

HOLD THE ROPE

GIVE TRUST

PROGRESS, NOT PERFECTION

Family

Kent Myers

19

Choose the Right Side

As John finished writing on the whiteboard, the whole room glanced over at the four remaining pieces of paper with enthusiasm. Sara was glowing with a huge smile on her face when she burst out, "I love this! Who's next?"

John Hill walked back to the table, his hands hovering over the four folded slips of paper on the table, finally picking one from the middle. He unfolded it and read out

Family

aloud the words, "Choose the right side." This was followed by mixed looks of confusion and curiosity.

After a long moment of silence, Emily, the clinic's receptionist, spoke up. "That one's mine," she said. "As some of you know, I have been returning home occasionally to check on my mom. She is getting older, and I just want to be there for her when I can. Three weeks ago, I went home to help her with a number of important decisions and to take care of some neglected tasks. It was a tough time.

"So, when the week was over and I was heading back, I was grateful to be sinking into my airplane seat for a much-needed respite. As passengers were boarding, a little boy brimming with excitement was making his way down the aisle, his Scooby Doo backpack bouncing with each step. Just as he reached my row, he twirled around and inadvertently spilled his drink on the lady in the aisle seat. While this could have easily escalated into a major ordeal, I was surprised by her reaction.

"The boy's mother was mortified, and the boy himself looked anxious about the mess he'd made. Yet, the woman simply smiled and reassured the mother, saying, 'No problem at all. I have three children, all grown now. I really miss those days of fun, excitement and joy.' The mother's relief and gratitude were palpable. Later, a flight attendant approached the woman to thank her for her kindness.

"That moment made me remember the words of my mom many years ago. She would say, 'While we can't always control things that happen to us, we can always choose how we *react* to them.'" With tears in her eyes, Emily continued, "My mom would refer me to a list that hung on our refrigerator door."

HATE has 4 letters, but so does **LOVE**
ENEMIES has 7 letters, but so does **FRIENDS**
LYING has 5 letters, but so does **TRUTH**
FAILURE has 7 letters, but so does **SUCCESS**
CRY has 3 letters, but so does **JOY**
NEGATIVITY has 10 letters, but so does **POSITIVITY**

"I can still hear her say, *'CHOOSE THE RIGHT SIDE.'*"

Family

The room was silent as every person intently focused on Emily's touching words.

Emily cleared her throat. "I love the quote from Charles Swindoll: '*Life is 10% what happens to you and 90% how you react to it.*' The reality is that we face these choices daily at work and in our personal lives. We have CHOICES in how we react to bad news, mishaps or even bad behavior. We are in control of our reactions, our words and our actions. I still think about that lady sitting on the aisle. I wonder how I would have reacted if it were me. She had a choice that night; instead of becoming frustrated, yelling and making the situation worse for the mother and the little boy, she responded with kindness, understanding and empathy. In that moment, she was an example and an inspiration to me and to everyone around. She inspired me and reminded me that it is all up to us! **Choose the 'right' side of the list.**"

Henry walked over and put a hand on Emily's shoulder. "Thank you for being that example of the right side of the list for us, Emily."

As John looked around the room, he knew there wasn't even any need to ask if this ought to be included in the common vocabulary. The looks on their faces, the tears in their eyes and the respectful silence in the room spoke volumes.

John walked to the board and slowly wrote:

HOLD THE ROPE

GIVE TRUST

PROGRESS, NOT PERFECTION

CHOOSE THE RIGHT SIDE

John turned, looked at Emily, and said, "That's for your mom and all those who have helped us understand that our words and actions *are* impactful, in every moment of every day."

Family

20

Assume Positive Intent

Now only three pieces of paper remained and just three voices were yet to be heard. John turned from the whiteboard and walked back to the table. He was amazed with the energy that had filled the room and the engagement of the staff as they created the new vocabulary of the culture.

John picked up a tightly folded piece of paper as it revealed the words: *Assume Positive Intent*. John smiled as he read it. "I love this one! Whose is this?"

Family

The stoic veteran nurse in the corner raised his hand. "It's a phrase that has had great significance in my life, but also one that I have struggled with," he said quietly. "May I share a story with you all?" he asked, looking around the room. Nods of agreement came from every corner. They had grown to appreciate Roger's wisdom and the calm presence he brought to their often-chaotic work environment.

"It wasn't ever easy for me to assume positive intent," Roger began. "In fact, there was a time when I was just as quick to judge and react as anyone else." He paused, remembering the pivotal moments that had shaped his approach. "Early in my career, I had a colleague named Stella. She was an excellent nurse, but we just couldn't see eye to eye. Our interactions were tense, filled with misunderstandings and assumptions. I believed she was out to undermine me, and I'm sure she felt the same about me."

Roger took a deep breath, the memory still vivid. "One day, we had a major disagreement over patient care. We both raised our voices and stormed off, convinced the other was in the wrong. It was then that I decided to seek advice from Dr. Matthews, an old mentor of mine. He listened patiently and then asked me a question that changed everything: 'Roger, have you ever considered that Stella might have positive intentions, just like you?'"

The room was silent as Roger continued, "I hadn't. I was so caught up in my own perspective that I never stopped to consider hers. Dr. Matthews explained the Fundamental Attribution Error to me—how we tend to attribute the actions of others to their *character* while blaming our own mistakes on *external* factors. He encouraged me to assume positive intent and to see the situation from Stella's point of view."

The team listened intently as Roger reached the turning point in his story. "The next day, I approached Stella and suggested we sit down and talk. I was nervous, but I wanted to try to understand her perspective. To my surprise, she agreed. During our conversation, I learned that Stella was under immense pressure at home. Her mother was ill and she was struggling to balance work and her personal life. She wasn't trying to undermine me, she was simply overwhelmed."

Family

Roger smiled, remembering the relief and connection that came from that conversation. "Assuming positive intent allowed us to see each other as allies rather than adversaries. It transformed our relationship. We started to support each other, and our teamwork improved dramatically. I learned that by giving people the benefit of the doubt you open the door to empathy and understanding."

He looked around the room, meeting the eyes of each of his colleagues. "This lesson didn't just change my relationship with Stella, it changed how I interacted with *everyone*. I started to assume that people had good intentions, even when their actions didn't seem to reflect that. It helped me build stronger relationships, both at work and in my personal life."

Roger's voice softened, filled with sincerity. "I know it's not always easy to assume positive intent, especially when we feel wronged or misunderstood, but I've found that it's a powerful way to navigate conflicts and build trust. It helps us see the bigger picture and understand the situational factors influencing others' behavior. Most importantly, it reminds us that we're all human—prone to making mistakes and having misunderstandings."

Emily raised her hand. "Roger, how do you manage to keep this mindset, especially on tough days?"

Roger chuckled softly. "It takes practice, Emily. It requires conscious effort and a willingness to pause before reacting. Whenever I feel myself getting frustrated or ready to judge, I take a moment to remind myself of the bigger picture. I ask myself, 'What could be going on in this person's life that I don't know about?' and 'How would I want to be treated if I were in their shoes?'"

He continued, "Over time, it becomes a habit. And the more you practice it, the more you see the positive impact it has on your relationships. It doesn't mean that you should ignore problems or avoid accountability, it means that you should address issues with empathy and understanding—creating a more supportive and collaborative environment."

Roger leaned back, his eyes reflecting the depth of his experiences. "Assuming positive intent has brought me peace

Family

and has strengthened my connections with others. It's a simple shift, but its impact is profound. I hope you all can see why I believe not only that these *words* should be a standard phrase within our clinic's common language, but that they all need to be followed up with *actions*."

The room was filled with a contemplative silence as they all absorbed Roger's words. They knew that in the fast-paced, high-stress world of healthcare, this simple yet powerful mindset could make all the difference.

John stepped forward. "So how do we feel about including this as part of our vocabulary?"

Everyone in the room nodded. As John approached the whiteboard, he glanced at Roger and said, "Thank you for sharing your heart, Roger," as he turned and wrote on the board:

HOLD THE ROPE

GIVE TRUST

PROGRESS, NOT PERFECTION

CHOOSE THE RIGHT SIDE

ASSUME POSITIVE INTENT

Kent Myers

Family

21

Positive Gossip

Now only two slips of paper remained. One had been folded loosely, exposing the word "gossip." As John glanced down at the table, he thought to himself, *this should be interesting.* As he began to unfold the paper, the whole phrase was revealed: "**Positive Gossip.**" He looked up and said,

"Not completely sure I understand this one: positive gossip. Which one of you two submitted this?"

Victoria, the clinic administrator, spoke up immediately. "That one is mine. When we were growing up, we referred to that as the "Thumper Rule." In the Disney movie *Bambi*, there is a scene when Bambi's cottontail companion, Thumper, is corrected by his mother after he makes a rude comment about Bambi. When his mother asks, 'Thumper, what did your father tell you?' he replies sweetly, 'If you don't have somethin' nice to say, don't say nuthin' at all.'"

It was almost as if Victoria went into "teacher mode." Her voice became clear and her face and eyes became focused. "When we think about the term 'gossip,' it is not typically positive thoughts that spring to mind. Most of our thoughts and memories go to negative comments or rumors about another. My own father wisely told me, 'Taking the coat off of someone else's back doesn't make mine any warmer.' He meant that tearing others down doesn't build us up—it actually brings all of us down together."

Family

Every person in the room was now fixed on Victoria's passionate words. She cleared her throat and began again. "Now, I know that the word 'gossip' usually has a bad connotation. But what if we could flip it on its head and use it for good? What if we practiced **POSITIVE GOSSIP**? Positive gossip is all about sharing uplifting, kind and appreciative stories about each other behind their backs. It's about spreading the good news and celebrating each other's successes and strengths."

Roger raised his hand. "Victoria, how can positive gossip really make a difference? Isn't it just another form of talking about people when they're not around?"

Victoria nodded thoughtfully. "That's a great question, Roger. The difference lies in the intent and the impact. Negative gossip can tear people down and create mistrust, but positive gossip does the opposite. It builds people up and fosters a culture of encouragement and mutual respect."

She paused, letting her words sink in before continuing. "Imagine hearing from a colleague that someone else praised your hard work or kindness when you weren't there to hear it yourself. It would make you feel appreciated and valued, wouldn't it? That's the power of positive gossip. It not only boosts morale, but also strengthens our sense of community."

A few heads nodded in agreement, and Victoria was encouraged enough to delve deeper. "I suggested making positive gossip part of our common vocabulary because it's a simple yet powerful way to reinforce our clinic's core values. When we talk positively about each other, it creates a ripple effect. People feel more motivated, more connected and more committed to their work and to their colleagues."

She glanced around the room, making eye contact with as many staff members as she could. "Think about the times you've heard someone say something nice about you. Didn't it brighten your day? Didn't it make you want to continue doing your best? By actively engaging in positive gossip, we can create a supportive environment where everyone feels seen and appreciated."

Family

Judy Walters raised her hand. "Victoria, can you give us some examples of how we can practice positive gossip in our daily interactions?"

Victoria smiled warmly. "Absolutely, Judy. It can be as simple as sharing a story about how a colleague went above and beyond for a patient, or mentioning how someone always has a positive attitude, even on the busiest days. You can also highlight a team's collaborative success or acknowledge a small act of kindness that made a big difference."

She paused, letting the staff absorb the idea. "The key is being genuine and specific. Positive gossip isn't about flattery or empty compliments, it's about recognizing and celebrating the real contributions and qualities of our colleagues. When we do this, we create a culture of appreciation that pervades every aspect of our work."

Roger leaned forward, a thoughtful expression on his face. "I can see how this aligns with our clinic's mission and values. It's a practical way to live out our commitment and to protect this culture of Family."

"Exactly," Victoria affirmed. "And it starts with each one of us. I encourage you all to give it a try. Start small and notice the difference it makes. Let's make positive gossip a cornerstone of our clinic's culture."

That was all that John needed to hear. He walked toward the board and as he did, he said, "Victoria, I see a passion in you that I haven't seen these last couple of days, and I like it." He then turned toward the whiteboard and added the phrase "Positive Gossip" to the list of common terminology. As John turned back around, he looked toward the table and said, "And then there was ONE," as his eyes turned toward Sara.

Family

22

Be Curious

Dr. Sara Tuttle didn't wait for John. She reached for the last piece of paper on the table and opened it up, laying the words on the table face up for everyone to see. Everyone in the room could clearly make out the words written in bold letters, "**Be Curious.**" At that moment, those words were living out on the faces of every staff member in the room; faces of bewilderment and curiosity.

Family

"These two simple words have had a profound impact on my life and are quite honestly my ask of each of you as we journey through the transition in this clinic. It is my hope that 'Be Curious' will be one of the phrases in our common language," she said humbly. She paused, letting the words sink in. "Curiosity is more than just a trait, it's a mindset. It's about never halting our pursuit of knowledge and understanding. In healthcare, this can make a world of difference."

Dr. Tuttle glanced around the room, making eye contact with her colleagues. "Let me share a story from early in my career. I was a young resident, and I had a patient with a set of symptoms that didn't quite add up. The easy thing to do would have been to follow the standard protocol, but something about the case piqued my curiosity. I dug deeper, asked more questions and consulted with specialists. Ultimately, we discovered an unusual diagnosis that saved the patient's life. If I hadn't stayed curious, that patient might not be with us today."

The room was silent, captivated by her story. "Curiosity drives us to ask the extra question, to go the extra mile. It keeps us learning and growing, which is essential in a field that is constantly evolving. By staying curious, we are ensured of providing the best possible care for our patients."

Dr. Tuttle's expression softened as she shifted the focus. "But curiosity isn't just about medical knowledge, it's also about our relationships with each other. When we stay curious about our colleagues, we strengthen our connections. We learn about their experiences, their perspectives and what drives them. This not only makes us better teammates, but also creates a supportive and collaborative work environment."

She took a step forward, her voice gentle but firm, "I encourage all of you to ask questions, to be open-minded, and to stay curious about the people you work with—especially with this transition. Let's create a culture where we are constantly learning from and about each other. When we understand and appreciate the unique contributions of our colleagues, we can work together more effectively and with greater empathy."

Family

Dr. Tuttle paused again, allowing her words to resonate. "Imagine a workplace where everyone is genuinely interested in each other's ideas and experiences—where we support each other's growth and celebrate our collective curiosity. This is the kind of environment I believe we can create."

She smiled, her eyes shining with conviction. "We have been in this meeting for almost an hour, and I have learned more about each of you in that time than in the weeks that I have been here."

The room erupted in applause and Dr. Tuttle felt a surge of hope and excitement. She knew that if they all embraced this mindset, this transition would prove to be a success for everyone involved. She could see the light at the end of the tunnel. She now understood the misconceptions and miscommunications surrounding her intentions and the future of the clinic.

John approached the whiteboard and added the final phrase to the list: "Be Curious." As he stepped back, the whole room looked on with amazement at the clarity of the future that was gained during the past hour regarding the path forward for the clinic. As John stepped back now, everyone could see the whole picture.

There was an electricity in the room that had been absent for months; ever since Dr. Henry Tuttle announced his plans to retire. Henry stood up with tears in his eyes and said, "Of all that we have accomplished over the many years, I have never been prouder to be a part of this clinic as I am at this every moment."

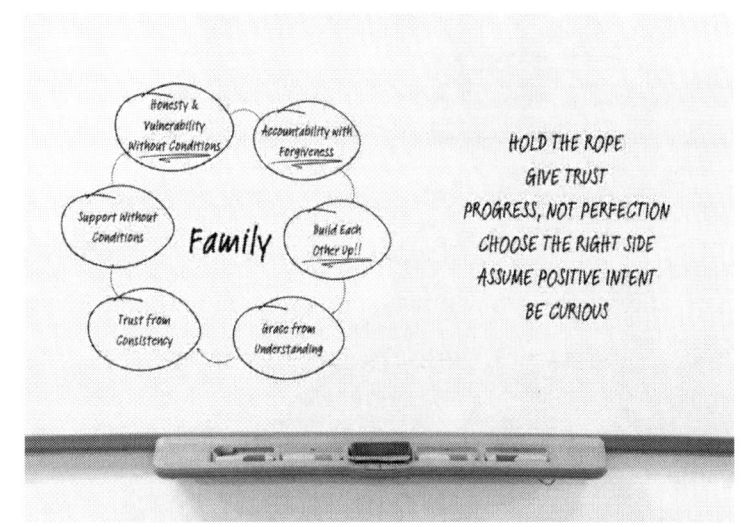

Family circle with surrounding elements: Honesty & Vulnerability Without Conditions, Accountability with Forgiveness, Build Each Other Up!!, Grace from Understanding, Trust from Consistency, Support Without Conditions.

HOLD THE ROPE
GIVE TRUST
PROGRESS, NOT PERFECTION
CHOOSE THE RIGHT SIDE
ASSUME POSITIVE INTENT
BE CURIOUS

Henry glanced over at John and continued, "John has always told me that there are two things to remember about culture: First, it is not complicated. Culture is simply that aggregation of attitudes and behaviors of any group of people; and second, those attitudes are most highly influenced—not by posters and presentations—but by the behaviors that we see in each other every day. I see the future of this clinic in what we have talked about this afternoon and now I feel encouraged, proud and very *comfortable* to be able to step away."

There was not a dry eye in the room as Henry finished speaking. Along with a contagious enthusiasm for the future, everyone also mourned the passing of the leadership baton and the thought of this clinic without Henry. As the meeting began to wrap up, each person paused on the way out to thank Henry for his unwavering care and his focus on the clinic's culture. They appreciated his dedication to preserving the rich history and traditions of the clinic while addressing the immediate needs of the present.

Everyone also stopped to share kind words of appreciation to Sara for her heart, leadership and desire to come home to this small town to continue the care that the Tuttle family had provided for decades.

After a few minutes the room had cleared except for John, Henry and Sara; it felt different. It seemed that thoughts and the tone had changed from looking anxiously at the past to confidently, calmly and clearly looking toward the future.

Family

23

My Work is Done Here

As the sun began to set, the light from the west conference room window cast a warm, calming glow over the room which seemed appropriate for the occasion. John, Henry and Sara all took a seat around the long table, emotionally drained from their recent roller coaster ride.

Henry leaned back in his chair, a mix of nostalgia and relief evident on his face. "I have to admit, John, I was skeptical that we would reach the point that we did this afternoon. I've poured my heart and soul into this place. The idea of handing it over... it was daunting."

John smiled, his eyes reflecting the compassion that had guided his efforts this week. "Change is always challenging, Henry, but what I found here is extraordinary. The sense of family, the genuine care everyone has for each other—it's rare, and it's something worth protecting."

Sara, sitting across from Henry, nodded in agreement. Her initial anxiety had given way to a newfound confidence. "John, your conversations with the staff have been transformative. The fears we had about losing our culture have turned into a shared understanding of what makes this clinic special. You've helped us see that."

Henry's expression softened as he looked at Sara. "I was worried that the care and support we've built here would be overshadowed by new leadership, new processes and new technology. But instead, you've shown that we share the same heart for our patients, for the staff and for this culture. I couldn't be more grateful. I trust you and I am so proud of you."

Family

Sara took a deep breath, her determination evident. "I promise to uphold the ideals that define this place. The concept of FAMILY will remain at the heart of everything we do. The new common language of culture you've introduced, John, has given us the tools to sustain and nurture those values."

John felt a sense of accomplishment. "I've always believed that words matter. They shape our attitudes and behaviors. By defining and embracing a common language, we've created a foundation that will support this clinic long into the future."

The three sat in comforting silence for a moment, fully absorbing the weight of their conversation. Finally, Henry broke the silence. "John, your clarity has been a gift. You've ensured that the essence of this clinic—the FAMILY—will endure. I can step down knowing that it's in good hands."

Sara reached out, placing a hand on Henry's arm. "And I'll carry forward what you've built, with a deep appreciation for the culture that makes us who we are. I love you, Dad."

As John stood, he was overcome by a profound sense of purpose and accomplishment. "This clinic is more than just a place of work, it's a community; it's a family. Families grow and adapt, but their core values and beliefs remain. With the clarity we've achieved together, I'm confident this clinic will continue to thrive. My work is done here, and I am going to get back to my retirement."

As they left the office, the sun fully illuminated the hallway, symbolizing the sunset of the past and the arrival of a new dawn for the clinic. The confusion and anxiety of the past week had given way to optimism and a shared commitment to protect and nurture the culture that bound them together. The future was bright, anchored by the strong foundation of FAMILY and the new common language that would guide them into the future.

Family

Kent Myers

24

Discussion Guide

Real learning, growth and relationship development happens in conversations. This discussion guide is to be a foundation of team conversations where we can learn together and about each other.

Culture is simply the aggregation of attitudes and behaviors of a group of people. We will always have culture, either by design or by default. When we think about the intentional and aspired future culture of your team or group,

Family

if you were to articulate that in one word, what would that one word be?

Kent Myers

Family

When we talk about trust, we know that trust comes from attitudinal, behavioral and operational consistency. What are a few things that we need to be consistent about every day?

Kent Myers

Family

When we think about supporting each other and "having each other's back," we just read about the five levels of support:

- <u>Level 1</u>: I won't throw you under the bus.
- <u>Level 2</u>: If you're in distress and you ask me for help, I'll agree to help.
- <u>Level 3</u>: If I see that you're in distress, I'll stop and volunteer my help.
- <u>Level 4</u>: I know where you're likely to need help and I'll ask if you're struggling and need my help. This includes looking for the inspiration in every idea and seeing the value in intention.
- <u>Level 5</u>: You are my "ride or die." No matter what's going on with me, I'm dedicated to your success. I will do what I can to care for you and bring out your best.

At what level are we at with those on our team? How do we get to level 5?

_____

_____

Kent Myers

Family

Kent Myers

We know the power of gratitude, appreciation and celebration of our successes. What might get in our way of these things and how do we overcome them?

Family

Familiarity of knowing each other and knowing what is going on in each other's lives. When we understand each other, we eliminate assumptions and give each other grace. The other side of this is that some people are more private. How do we balance boundaries of personal lives and caring for others by understanding them?

Family

Creating a psychologically safe environment is imperative for people to share and be open. How do we create this type of environment and combat the enemies of safety such as gossip and grudges?

Family

Exercise: Our words matter in the leadership shadow that we cast. With your team, discuss and create your own "Common Language of Culture." What are the phrases we use or those that support our aspired culture?

Family

Made in the USA
Columbia, SC
17 October 2024

451ad131-c742-4f5b-89de-7a9a8acd9bedR01